Sports Illustrated

P R E S E N T S

2006 ROSE BOWL | *QB Vince Young*

TEXAS
LONGHORNS
F O O T B A L L

INTRODUCTION BY DAN JENKINS

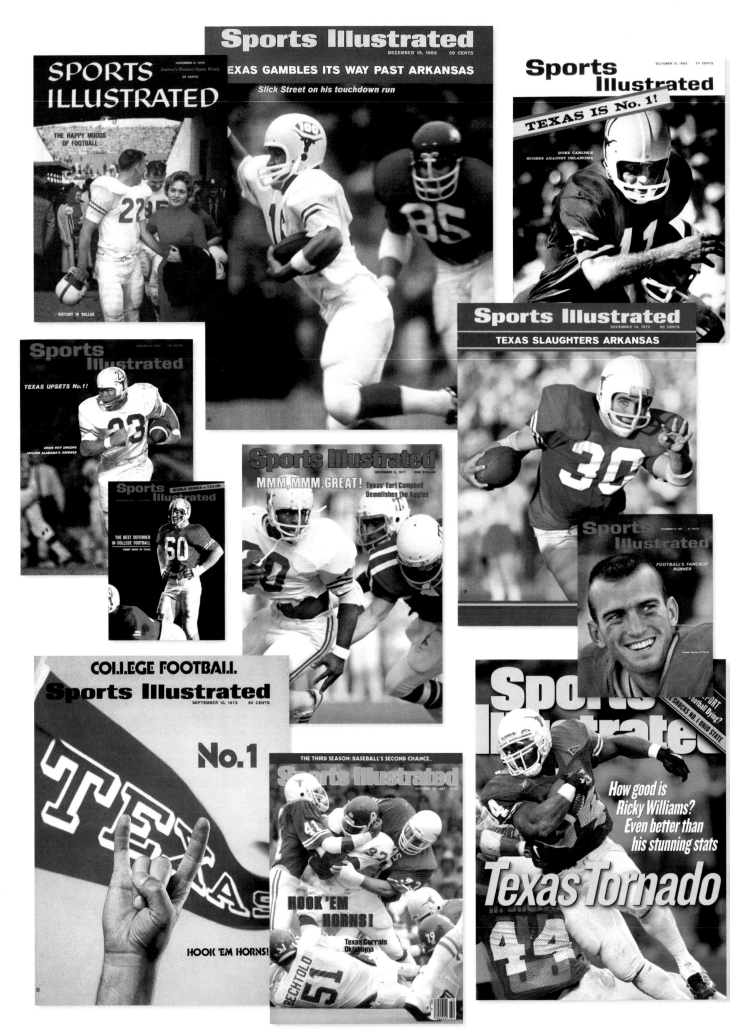

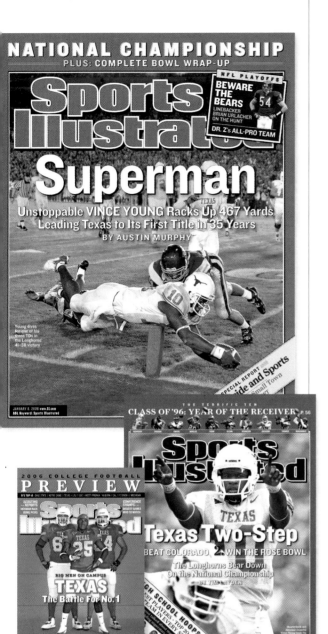

Sports Illustrated

CONTENTS

P R E S E N T S

COVER PHOTOGRAPH: UNIVERSITY OF TEXAS FRONT COVER FLAP: AUSTIN HISTORY CENTER, AUSTIN PUBLIC LIBRARY FRONT ENDPAPER: BETTMANN/CORBIS (BILLY DALE SCORES THE GAME-WINNING TD IN THE 1970 COTTON BOWL) TITLE PAGE: JOHN BIEVER CONTENTS COVER PHOTOGRAPHS: NEIL LEIFER (4); DARREN CARROLL (2); WALTER IOOSS JR. (2); ROBERT BECK; JOHN BIEVER; ICON SMI; HEINZ KLUETMEIER; PETER READ MILLER; MARVIN E. NEWMAN; LAWRENCE SCHILLER; TONY TRIOLO BACK ENDPAPER: WESLEY HITT/GETTY IMAGES BACK COVER FLAP: CENTER FOR AMERICAN HISTORY, UNIVERSITY OF TEXAS; BRIAN BAHR/GETTY IMAGES; JOHN BIEVER; WALTER IOOSS JR; NEIL LEIFER; GREG NELSON; SUZANNE PLUNKETT/AP; BOB ROSATO; FRANK SCHERSCHEL; ERIC SCHWEIKARDT; UNIVERSITY OF TEXAS BACK COVER: DARREN CARROLL (2); JAMES DRAKE (2); MARVIN E. NEWMAN (2); UNIVERSITY OF TEXAS (2); AP; ROBERT BECK; CENTER FOR AMERICAN HISTORY, UNIVERSITY OF TEXAS; RICH CLARKSON; WALTER IOOSS JR.; HEINZ KLUETMEIER; DAVID E. KLUTHO; KIRBY LEE/IMAGE OF SPORT/US PRESSWIRE; NEIL LEIFER; PETER READ MILLER; GREG NELSON; L.M. OTERO/AP; HY PESKIN; FRANK SCHERSCHEL; LAWRENCE SCHILLER; TONY TOMSIC

SPORTS ILLUSTRATED GROUP
Editor Terry McDonell **President** Mark Ford **Vice President, Consumer Marketing** John Reese

SPORTS ILLUSTRATED PRESENTS
Editor Neil Cohen **Creative Director** Craig Gartner **Senior Editors** Trisha Blackmar, Richard O'Brien (PROJECT EDITOR)
Photo Editor Jeffrey Weig **Editorial Manager** Pamela Ann Roberts **Staff Editor** David Sabino **Associate Editor** Gene Menez
Senior Writers Tim Layden, Austin Murphy **Staff Writer** Mark Beech **Writer-Reporter**
Adam Duerson **Reporters** Elizabeth McGarr, Jordan Conn, Anne Larimer Hart, Matt Lawyue **Deputy Art Director**
Karen Meneghin **Associate Photo Editor** Kari Stein **Copy Editors** Denis Johnston, Richard McAdams (DEPUTY), Jill Jaroff,
Kevin Kerr, Nancy Ramsey, Bernice Rohret, Anthony Scheitinger, John Shostrom **Director of Imaging** Geoffrey A. Michaud
Managers Dan Larkin, Robert M. Thompson **Special Contributor** Dan Jenkins

TIME INC. HOME ENTERTAINMENT
Publisher Richard Fraiman **General Manager** Steven Sandonato **Executive Director, Marketing Services** Carol Pittard
Director, Retail & Special Sales Tom Mifsud **Director, New Product Development** Peter Harper **Assistant Director, Bookazine Marketing**
Laura Adam **Assistant Publishing Director, Brand Marketing** Joy Butts **Associate Counsel** Helen Wan **Brand & Licensing Manager**
Alexandra Bliss **Design & Prepress Manager** Anne-Michelle Gallero **Book Production Manager** Susan Chodakiewicz **Associate Brand**
Manager Allison Parker **Special Thanks:** Christine Austin, Glenn Buonocore, Jim Childs, Rose Cirrincione, Jacqueline Fitzgerald,
Lauren Hall, Jennifer Jacobs, Suzanne Janso, Brynn Joyce, Mona Li, Robert Marasco, Amy Migliaccio, Brooke Reger,
Dave Rozzelle, Ilene Schreider, Adriana Tierno, Alex Voznesenskiy, Sydney Webber

◄ To order photo reprints of your favorite SI covers, go to **SIcovers.com**

THE HEART

THE AUTHOR RECALLS A COACHING
GREATEST ERA, AND CELEBRATES THE

OF TEXAS

HERO WHO FORGED THE LONGHORNS' EXCELLENCE THAT LIVES ON | BY DAN JENKINS

DARRELL ROYAL IS THE ENTIRE REASON WHY SO MANY University of Texas football fans still cling to the hope that the cheese in their Tex-Mex enchiladas will come out burnt orange. I can think of no form of flattery that would please him more. ¶ Coach Royal made a boldface, italicized, underlined impression on people. He became my alltime hero among coaching immortals and was, year in and year out, an absolute joy for a sportswriter to cover as he turned Texas into a locomotive on the national football landscape. ¶ As for the burnt orange, Royal brought it back from the late 1920s and early 1930s to make it the official Texas color before the 1962 season. In what was his sixth season as the Longhorns' coach, he'd decided he wanted

Even pre-Royal, Texas had a regal tradition with the likes of the versatile Koy (far left), Crain (99) and Layden (11)—who along with teammates made their mark on LIFE—and the Blond Bomber (41). Bible (far right) got the Longhorns on the board in the early '40s.

the team to have its own distinctive look. Not to be confused with Tennessee, Clemson, Oklahoma State or any other school that wore bright orange.

Some thought—myself included—that there was another reason. Burnt orange jerseys were the same color as the football, and if you were running a sleight-of-hand T-formation offense, well....

The day I suggested this to Darrell, he only grinned slightly. Which meant that I was either correct or must have been joking.

There was winning football at Texas before Darrell Royal, of course, even before Dana X. Bible, and there is winning football today in Austin during this remarkable reign of Mack Brown. But it's the Royal years of the late 1950s through the mid-1970s that are still fondled

with the most affection by followers of the Longhorns.

And why not? Three national championships, two near-national championships, 11 Southwest Conference titles, 16 bowl teams, 26 first-team All-Americas, a Heisman Trophy winner . . . that'll do it for most folks.

I should also mention three other fairly huge accomplishments.

One, Royal never lost a game to Bear Bryant, arguably the greatest coach who ever motivated a locker room. Royal was 3-0-1 against Bear.

Two, it's surprising to look back and realize that in that madcap series of dramatic shootouts with Frank Broyles and the Arkansas Razorbacks, which were often nail-bitingly close, Darrell won 14 and lost only five.

And three, after Royal took over the Longhorns, in

1957, he immediately went 6–1 against Oklahoma and his old coach, Bud Wilkinson, thus hastening Wilkinson's retirement.

Royal had recognized that one of his immediate chores at Texas would be to "turn that thing around down in Dallas," as he put it. Meaning the annual Red River rivalry—the Texas-OU game—in the Cotton Bowl. When Darrell got to Austin, the Longhorns had lost eight of their past nine games to the hated Sooners.

But Royal knew he had a little tradition going for him. The University of Texas had a rich football history, a big reputation and a vast alumni base swelled with a furious pride. As Darrell said to a few of us after accepting the job

He could build on the national prominence achieved under coach D.X. Bible shortly before World War II.

It took Bible awhile after he left Nebraska for Austin. Bible's first two teams at Texas went 2-6-1 in 1937 and 1–8 in 1938. This inspired Wilbur Evans, an Austin sportswriter at the time, to label the program, Ali Bible and the Forty Sieves.

That line achieved immortality among sports scribes, but Bible managed to overcome it.

It was in the last conference game of the 1940 season that Bible's five-year plan started to kick in. The Longhorns scored one of the greatest college football upsets of all time when they defeated unbeaten Texas A&M, the defending

 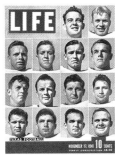  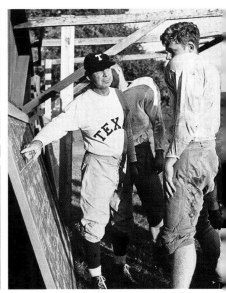

in Austin, "It's not like I've been hired to coach Step in It U. I've played against these people when they were mad. What I've got to do is make 'em mad again."

He knew there was a lot of tradition to build on. He could build on the great 1920 team that was undefeated (9–0) and led by a quaint group of guys with names out of a gangster movie—Rats Watson, Hook McCullough, Swede Swenson, Maxey Hart and Icky Elam.

He could build on the burnt-orange teams of coach Clyde Littlefield that terrorized the Southwest Conference from 1928 through 1933 and once produced an all-conference backfield that featured big Ernie Koy, who could do it all; Harrison Stafford, the halfback known for his fierce blocking; and the dazzling broken-field running of Bohn Hilliard, the Orange Flash, who conveniently came from Orange, Texas.

national champion, 7–0. This was an A&M team led by the legendary Jarrin' John Kimbrough. The Aggies were riding a 19-game winning streak, and the jarring upset knocked them out of a certain invitation to the Rose Bowl.

The Longhorns scored in the first 58 seconds that day on two long passes and a one-yard plunge. Fullback Pistol Pete Layden, a junior from Dallas, tossed a 32-yard pass to the tailback Jack Crain, the Nocona Nugget, and then a 32-yard pass to his wingback, Noble Doss from Temple, Texas, who made a circus catch and toppled out-of-bounds on the A&M one. On the next play Layden punched it over and Crain booted the extra point.

The Aggies spent the following 59 minutes driving into Texas territory but failed to score, largely due to their uncharacteristic habit of throwing intercepted passes, five in all that Thanksgiving afternoon. It's still remembered as the day the Texas Aggies cornered the market on Kleenex.

A year later those same Longhorns, now seniors, would command even more national attention. After winning their first six games by trouncing Colorado 34–6, LSU 34–0, Oklahoma 40–7, Arkansas 48–14, Rice 40–0 and SMU 34–0, the Steers seized the nation's No. 1 ranking, and 14 of them wound up on the Nov. 17, 1941, cover of LIFE magazine. Cover billing: TEXAS FOOTBALL.

This was a monumental thing for the Longhorns as well as the Southwest Conference, but maybe you have to be of a certain age to appreciate the influence that

No. 2 in the rankings, this time by 23–0, and then brutally walloped Oregon 71–7.

This prompted the Williamson rating system, second only to the AP poll in importance at the time, to assess the whole season and declare Texas the national champion.

Between that era and the arrival of Royal and his creations—the burnt-orange jerseys, the now-familiar steer's-head logo and eventually the wishbone offense—Texas fans had little to brag about other than the pitching arm and scene-stealing exploits of All-America quarterback Bobby Layne. Sweet Bobby, as he often referred to himself, or the Blond Bomber, as he was known to sportswriters throughout his four seasons, from 1944 through 1947.

Under Royal (left, riding high after Texas topped Arkansas in 1970 to clinch the national title) the Longhorns dominated their rivals, going 3-0-1 against Alabama (including an Orange Bowl win in '65, top right) and 14–5 against the Razorbacks (with a thriller in '69, bottom).

LIFE had in those pretelevision days. So let's enshrine the cover boys again—top row: end Wally Scott, blocking back Vern Martin; second row: reserve tailback Spec Sanders, All-America end Mal Kutner, tackle Julian Garrett, center Henry Harkins; third row: wingback Noble Doss, reserve fullback R. L. Harkins, end Preston Flanagan, All-America guard Chal Daniel; bottom row: guard Buddy Jungmichel, fullback Pete Layden, tackle Bo Cohenour, tailback Jack Crain.

The '41 Longhorns finished the season with an 8-1-1 record after suffering a 7–7 tie with Baylor and a 14–7 loss to TCU in the seventh and eighth games, largely due to injuries—both upsets occurring in the last minute of play—but they finished with a flourish. They again blasted an undefeated Texas A&M team (8–0), which had climbed to

It seems safe to say that there was never a more revered, larger-than-life presence at the University of Texas than Bobby Layne—until Darrell Royal came along.

Darrell not only brought winning to Texas but along with it came his Royalisms, words of wisdom that have practically been carved into granite. Explaining his conservative approach on offense and his reliance on defense and the kicking game, he delivered the famous line, "Three things can happen when you throw a forward pass, and two of 'em are bad."

A cornerstone of his coaching philosophy went like this: "Luck is when preparation meets opportunity."

He wanted his running backs to drive for the end zone like they're sure "that's where the groceries are."

And when he won his first national championship, in

1963, the unbeaten Longhorns squeaked by Texas A&M in their final game, prevailing on a late touchdown drive, 15–13, and prompting a sportswriter to comment that it was "kind of an ugly win." Royal responded with the same thing he'd said to a Longhorns player who'd moaned that his current girlfriend was somewhat ugly.

The coach said, "Yeah, but Ole Ugly is better than Ole Nuthin'."

Indeed, Royal made such a lasting impression in Austin that after his retirement following the 1976 season, the university went through 21 years and three coaches—Fred Akers, David McWilliams, and John Mackovic—trying to find another icon. With Darrell's help they finally found

Rose Bowl his Horns came back with a 13–0 record and the national championship of 2005 after edging Southern California 41–38 in one of the greatest college games ever played.

It might have been appropriate for the trophy to be sawed in two and half of it given to Vince Young, the big, fast, dominating Texas quarterback, an All-America who performed at times like he must have come from another planet.

Mack had recruited Vince Young, which was one reason why Brown quickly became known as Coach February to those who follow the Texas high school recruiting wars.

Since Brown's arrival, in 1998, Longhorns football has bloomed again. With Royal at his side (bottom right), the new coach brought in the stars, none brighter than Young (10), whose heroics in the 2006 Rose Bowl gave Texas its fourth national championship.

him before the 1998 season, a guy named Mack Brown, a guy who could charm the media, handle the orange bloods, recruit like a scoundrel and even win a few football games.

Mack has owned several chunks of the Big 12 Conference since he arrived in Austin, at least the parts that don't belong to Oklahoma. He's made the Longhorns a permanent fixture in bowl games. In his 11 seasons he has yet to win fewer than nine games—and five times he's won 11 or more.

Among other things he's taken the Longhorns to the Rose Bowl twice, in the 2004 and '05 seasons, and the only other school from the state of Texas that has been to Pasadena for a postseason game was the 1935 SMU team. It was quite a wait. On Mack's second trip to the

But the best thing Mack Brown has done was bring Darrell Royal back into the program.

Royal had been instrumental in recommending Brown for the job, and before Mack accepted the challenge, he said to Darrell, "Coach, if I do this, I'm going to need your help."

Royal's reply was, "I'm not looking for a full-time job, but I'll help you any way I can. The problem with the Texas football program is that it's been like a box of BBs that scattered all over the place when somebody dropped them on the floor. Everybody is going in a different direction. Your job is to get the BBs back in the box."

With Darrell Royal as a priceless resource and a valued friend, the evidence indicates that Mack Brown has picked up all those little devils off the floor. □

THE TRE

THE LONGHORNS HAVE BEEN PLAYING FOOTBALL SINCE 1893 and rank as the second-winningest program in the history of the NCAA (and they are closing in fast on No. 1 Michigan). So, as one can imagine, it takes several Texas-sized trophy cases to display all the artifacts collected over

1963

Defensive lineman Scott Appleton wore number 70

1965

Tommy Nobis's 60 was worn by later LBs in his honor

1947

No one else could fill Bobby Layne's letter jacket

A S U R E S

the years. From jerseys to leather helmets, from cleats to whistles and from game balls to national-championship rings, there are countless memories in this memorabilia. There's no question that when it comes to locating college football treasures, Texas marks the spot. — COMPILED BY GENE MENEZ

Photographs by DARREN CARROLL

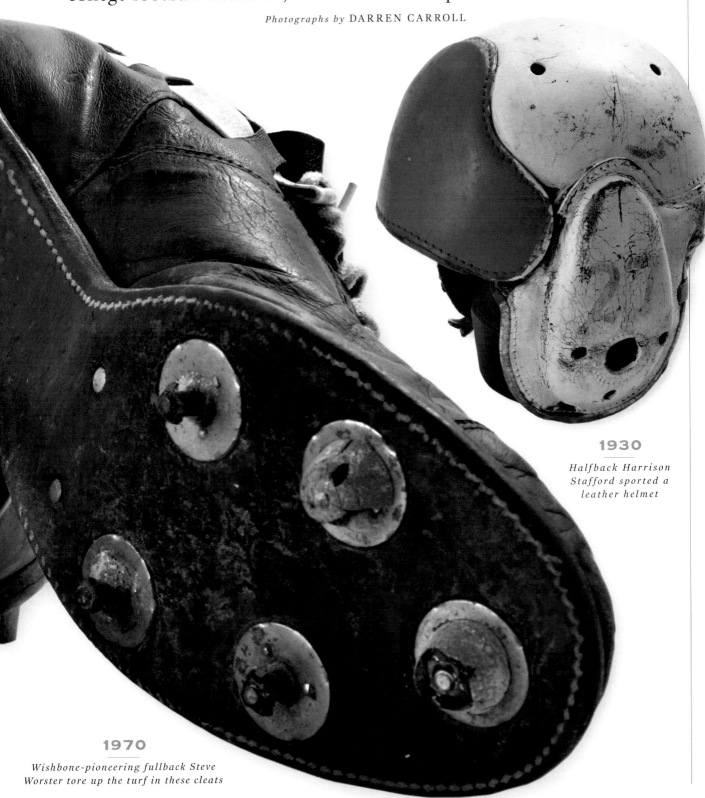

1930

Halfback Harrison Stafford sported a leather helmet

1970

Wishbone-pioneering fullback Steve Worster tore up the turf in these cleats

1972

*Darrell Royal's
Coach of the Year medallion*

1981

*Defensive tackle Kenneth
Sims's Lombardi Award*

2005

*Quarterback Vince Young's
Davey O'Brien Award*

TEXAS-OKLA
TO BE HEL

1929	TEXAS	21	OKLAHOMA	0
1930	TEXAS	17	OKLAHOMA	7
1931	TEXAS	3	OKLAHOMA	0
1932	TEXAS	17	OKLAHOMA	10
1933	TEXAS	0	OKLAHOMA	9
1934	TEXAS	19	OKLAHOMA	0
1935	TEXAS	12	OKLAHOMA	7
1936	TEXAS	6	OKLAHOMA	0
1937	TEXAS	7	OKLAHOMA	7
1938	TEXAS	0	OKLAHOMA	13
1939	TEXAS	12	OKLAHOMA	24
1940	TEXAS	19	OKLAHOMA	16
1941	TEXAS	40	OKLAHOMA	7
1942	TEXAS	7	OKLAHOMA	0
1943	TEXAS	13	OKLAHOMA	7
1944	TEXAS	20	OKLAHOMA	7
1945	TEXAS	12	OKLAHOMA	7
1946	TEXAS	20	OKLAHOMA	13
1947	TEXAS	34	OKLAHOMA	14
1948	TEXAS	14	OKLAHOMA	20

THE S

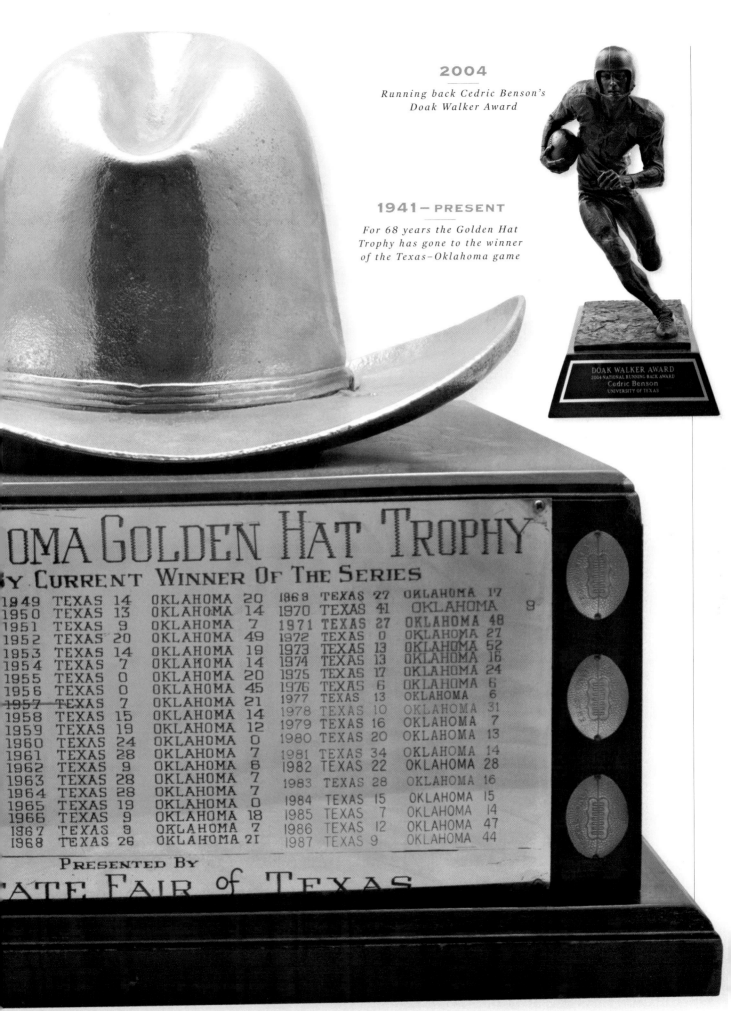

2004

*Running back Cedric Benson's
Doak Walker Award*

1941–PRESENT

*For 68 years the Golden Hat
Trophy has gone to the winner
of the Texas–Oklahoma game*

DOAK WALKER AWARD
2004 NATIONAL RUNNING BACK AWARD
Cedric Benson
UNIVERSITY OF TEXAS

OMA GOLDEN HAT TROPHY

BY CURRENT WINNER OF THE SERIES

1949	TEXAS	14	OKLAHOMA	20	1868	TEXAS	27	OKLAHOMA	17
1950	TEXAS	13	OKLAHOMA	14	1970	TEXAS	41	OKLAHOMA	9
1951	TEXAS	9	OKLAHOMA	7	1971	TEXAS	27	OKLAHOMA	48
1952	TEXAS	20	OKLAHOMA	49	1972	TEXAS	0	OKLAHOMA	27
1953	TEXAS	14	OKLAHOMA	19	1973	TEXAS	13	OKLAHOMA	52
1954	TEXAS	7	OKLAHOMA	14	1974	TEXAS	13	OKLAHOMA	16
1955	TEXAS	0	OKLAHOMA	20	1975	TEXAS	17	OKLAHOMA	24
1956	TEXAS	0	OKLAHOMA	45	1976	TEXAS	6	OKLAHOMA	6
1957	TEXAS	7	OKLAHOMA	21	1977	TEXAS	13	OKLAHOMA	6
1958	TEXAS	15	OKLAHOMA	14	1978	TEXAS	10	OKLAHOMA	31
1959	TEXAS	19	OKLAHOMA	12	1979	TEXAS	16	OKLAHOMA	7
1960	TEXAS	24	OKLAHOMA	0	1980	TEXAS	20	OKLAHOMA	13
1961	TEXAS	28	OKLAHOMA	7	1981	TEXAS	34	OKLAHOMA	14
1962	TEXAS	9	OKLAHOMA	6	1982	TEXAS	22	OKLAHOMA	28
1963	TEXAS	28	OKLAHOMA	7	1983	TEXAS	28	OKLAHOMA	16
1964	TEXAS	28	OKLAHOMA	7				
1965	TEXAS	19	OKLAHOMA	0	1984	TEXAS	15	OKLAHOMA	15
1966	TEXAS	9	OKLAHOMA	18	1985	TEXAS	7	OKLAHOMA	14
1967	TEXAS	9	OKLAHOMA	7	1986	TEXAS	12	OKLAHOMA	47
1968	TEXAS	26	OKLAHOMA	21	1987	TEXAS	9	OKLAHOMA	44

PRESENTED BY

ATE FAIR of TEXAS

2006

Football commemorating Texas's four national titles, signed by Darrell Royal and Mack Brown

1963

Football signed by members of the 1963 national championship team

2009

Coach Mack Brown's whistle keeps the current Longhorns moving

2006

Bronze football commemorating that year's Rose Bowl victory

2005

*Mack Brown's national
championship ring*

1969

*Offensive backfield coach
Emory Bellard's national
championship ring*

2005

*Mack Brown's
Rose Bowl champions ring*

20 HISTORIC MOMENTS

A RUN UP THE MIDDLE THROUGH 116 YEARS OF THE
FIRSTS, THE FINEST AND THE FUN IN TEXAS FOOTBALL

BY ELIZABETH McGARR

IF YOU'RE A TEXAS FOOTBALL FAN, YOU SURELY HAVE A
favorite moment, one that stands out among the pep rallies, the heart-
stopping wins and the blowouts. You could have been a kid holding
pom-poms, a student screaming your head off in Memorial Stadium
or a proud Texas Ex, still dressed in orange from head to toe. Maybe
your favorite memory was the first time you saw the Tower lit orange
after a win. Or when you, your father and grandfather watched James
Brown roll left in the Big 12 championship game—from your couch in
Dallas. Maybe it was when center Ryan Fiebiger took the time to pose
for a photo with you before the 1997 UCLA game. (On second thought,
maybe it's better to forget that one.) Or when LenDale White didn't
make that first down in the fourth quarter of the 2006 Rose Bowl.
Memories fade, but the truly great moments endure. Here are 20
that shaped the program's history and helped make the university
and its loyal, ever-growing fan base what they are today. ▶ ▶ ▶

Dedicated on Thanksgiving 1924 (left), Memorial Stadium fit Texas to a T.

◄ *Photograph by* AUSTIN HISTORY CENTER, AUSTIN PUBLIC LIBRARY

OPENING KICKOFF

UPON HEARING THAT THE UNIVERSITY OF TEXAS HAD formed a football team, the Dallas Foot Ball Club (calling themselves "the champions of Texas"), challenged the fledgling UT squad to a game on Nov. 30, 1893, at Fairgrounds Park in Dallas. A local haberdashery, Harrell & Wilcox, lent the Austin players $100 for room and board, and a railroad ticket agent gave them round-trip tickets. It may not have been pretty, but the Texas team beat Dallas 18–16 that Thanksgiving Day. A reporter for *The Dallas Morning News* wrote, "To a man who has never heard of Walter Camp and doesn't know a half-back from a tackle, the professional game of foot ball looks very much like an Indian wrestling match with a lot of running thrown in."

STRIKE UP THE BAND

GIVEN A FEW HOURS TO WRITE A SONG FOR THE Cowboy Minstrel Show in 1903, UT student John Sinclair borrowed a favorite phrase from university president Colonel Prather and a favorite tune, *I've Been Working on the Railroad*, and came up with *The Eyes of Texas*, which would soon be adopted as the school's alma mater. Sinclair knew that Prather—who had attended Washington and Lee, where he heard Gen. Robert E. Lee tell students that "the eyes of the South are upon you"—liked to remind students in Austin, "The eyes of Texas are upon you." All the live long day.

NAME THAT TEAM

UNTIL THE BEGINNING OF THE 20TH CENTURY THE Texas football teams were known as Varsity. Scribes began occasionally referring to the team as the Long Horns beginning in 1900, and *Daily Texan* sportswriter D.A. Frank first used the nickname in an '03 article after editor Alex Weisburg told his staff to use the moniker to refer to every school sports team in the hope that it would catch on. It did, gradually, and after future regent H.J. Lutcher Stark gave the football team blankets stitched with TEXAS LONGHORNS in 1913, the nickname became widely used.

NO BUM STEER

SOME SAY HE WAS NAMED FOR A POPULAR BEER. SOME say his name was a play on the word *beeve*, a slang term for a steer. The most colorful story of how the Texas mascot got his name involves a branding iron and a few mischievous Texas A&M students. In 1916, after losing to Texas, they kidnapped the mascot and branded him with the score of the previous year's game, which the Aggies had won 13–0. The steer returned to campus, and some creative Texas students changed the 13 to a B and the dash to an E, and stuck a V before the zero: BEVO. The name stuck.

IF YOU BUILD IT, . . .

CLARK FIELD JUST WASN'T GOING TO CUT IT ANYMORE. The wooden seats at the Texas football stadium couldn't hold the more than 20,000 fans who attended the 1922 Texas A&M game, and by the following December athletic

Texas took up the ball for the first time in 1893 (right). The Varsity, as the team was then called, debuted with a win. Littlefield (above) introduced burnt orange.

director Theo Bellmont had obtained approval from the Board of Regents to build a 27,000-seat concrete stadium. Excavation began on April 1, 1924, and the Longhorns played their first game on Nov. 8, against Baylor. At the A&M game on Thanksgiving Day the university held its dedication ceremony before 35,000 fans, and Governor Pat Neff officially christened Memorial Stadium, dedicating it to the nearly 200,000 Texans who had served in World War I. In 1996 the stadium was rededicated and officially named Darrell K Royal–Texas Memorial Stadium, which now holds 100,119.

LIVING COLOR

BEFORE THE 1928 SEASON SECOND-YEAR HEAD COACH Clyde Littlefield decided to do something about the bright orange jerseys his team wore. After all, they began to fade to yellow after repeated washings and led opponents to refer to the players as "yellow-bellies." Littlefield, who had earned 12 varsity letters while a student at Texas, consulted a friend working at the O'Shea Knitting Mills in Chicago who helped him concoct the perfect shade of dye: burnt orange. During World War II the dye was no longer being shipped from Germany, so the Texas squad again wore the bright-orange jerseys and did so until 1962, when Darrell Royal brought the color back.

OUTFIGHTING THE IRISH

IT WAS FITTING THAT FIRST-YEAR COACH JACK Chevigny, who had played at Notre Dame for Knute Rockne himself, would lead the Longhorns north to take on his alma mater in October 1934. He would coach at Texas for only

No bull, Bevo got his name in 1916 when Texas students tidied up an Aggie branding (left). In '40 Doss (below) proved nothing's impossible when you believe.

three seasons, but Chevigny delivered the biggest win in the program's history when he coached the Longhorns to a 7–6 upset of the Fighting Irish in South Bend. Texas end Jack Gray recovered the ball on the Notre Dame 18-yard line after the Irish fumbled the opening kickoff; four plays later halfback Bohn Hilliard's eight-yard touchdown run and extra-point kick gave the Longhorns the winning margin. It was the first time in three attempts that Texas had beaten Notre Dame, and the win vaulted UT into the national spotlight.

DOING THE IMPOSSIBLE

NOW KNOWN SIMPLY AS THE IMPOSSIBLE CATCH, wingback Noble Doss's over-the-shoulder, 32-yard grab on the third play of the Texas A&M game in 1940 set up what would turn out to be the winning touchdown. Spurred on by coach Dana X. Bible's pregame reading of Edgar Guest's poem *It Can Be Done* ("Just start to sing as you tackle the thing/That 'cannot be done,' and you'll do it"), the Longhorns upset the defending national champion Aggies 7–0 and extended their perfect record against their rivals at Memorial Stadium to 9–0.

EXPRESS LAYNE

UNDER COACH BIBLE, THE LONGHORNS WON THREE Southwest Conference championships, including in 1945, despite being without Bobby Layne for the first six games of the season before he was discharged by the Merchant Marine. Layne played halfback and fullback in '45, and he helped the Horns cap the season with a 40–27 Cotton Bowl win over Missouri, accounting for all of the Texas points that day as he ran for three touchdowns, passed for two, caught one and kicked four extra points. Missouri coach Chauncey Simpson was asked after the game why his Tigers hadn't performed better, "Too much Layne," he said. It was the second of four All-SWC seasons for Layne, who had been recruited to play baseball in Austin and who, as a four-time All-SWC pitcher, never lost a conference game.

SIGN OF THE TIMES

HEAD CHEERLEADER HARLEY CLARK INTRODUCED the Hook 'Em Horns hand signal at a pep rally in 1955. Classmate Henry Pitts had given him the idea, and Clark taught it to students gathered at Gregory Gym the day before the Horns played No. 8 TCU. Texas lost to the Horned Frogs 47–20, but the idea endured. Eighteen years later the gesture made the cover of SI when the Horns were tabbed as the preseason No. 1, and in 1997 SI ranked Hook 'Em Horns as the best hand signal in the country.

ROYAL WELCOME

RUMORS WERE SWIRLING ABOUT WHOM BIBLE, now athletic director, would hire to replace head coach Ed Price after the 1956 team had finished with the worst record in the program's history (1–9). Would it be Georgia Tech's Bobby Dodd? Notre Dame's Frank Leahy? Michigan State's Duffy Daugherty? "Stories were being spread about them coming to Texas," Royal told Texas historian John Wheat years later. "Mr. Bible wanted this to be handled differently. So he asked me to travel under an assumed name. I traveled under the name of Jim Pittman, who was my assistant coach at the University of Washington." Fewer than five hours after he arrived on campus, the 32-year-old Royal had a job, and Texas had a coach who would bring three national titles to the university in 20 years.

BAD TO THE 'BONE

THE FORMATION DIDN'T HAVE A FANCY NAME AT FIRST, but the alignment that Texas backfield coach Emory Bellard cooked up with Royal and the coaching staff before the 1968 season ended up being one of the greatest offensive innovations the game had seen and would win the Longhorns two national titles, in '69 and '70. Named by Houston sportswriter Mickey Herskowitz, the wishbone was a triple-option offense that placed the members of the backfield in a Y-shaped formation with the fullback directly behind the quarterback and the halfbacks split to the left and right five yards behind the QB. Asked nearly 30 years later about people saying that the wishbone might have run its course, Royal replied, "Oh, hell yes. They say that you can't come from behind [with the wishbone], that it's not any good when you're behind with two minutes to go. My rebuttal is that you're supposed to be doing something the first 58 minutes."

PASS PERFECT

THE PLAY HAD FAILED SEVERAL TIMES DURING THE 1969 season, but Royal had a hunch that Right 53 Veer Pass would work in the fourth quarter against No. 2 Arkansas on Dec. 6 of that year, with the top-ranked Longhorns down 14–8 and facing fourth-and-three from their own 43-yard line. He sent quarterback James Street into the game with the play, which called for the tight end, Randy Peschel, to go deep. "James had said in the huddle, 'If you can't get behind [the defender], just get enough for a first down,'" recalls Peschel, now 60. "I remember planting my foot to go deep, and I hoped we were on the same page." They were, and Peschel hauled in the pass for a 44-yard gain. Two plays later halfback Jim Bertelsen scored, and the extra point put the Longhorns up for good, capping their undefeated season and prompting President Richard Nixon, who was in attendance, to declare them the national champions. Said Nixon in the locker room before handing the championship plaque to Royal and the Longhorns, "This was one of the greatest games of all times."

FREDDIE STEINMARK'S BATTLE

NO ONE KNEW AT THE TIME JUST HOW GRITTY FREDDIE Steinmark's performance had been in the 1969 Arkansas game. Six days later he was told that bone cancer had been causing the pain he had been feeling in his left leg and that the leg would have to be amputated. "The doctors said he was in such great shape physically," then backfield coach Fred Akers told writer Terry Frei. "That was the only thing that kept him out there. They felt a lesser man's leg might have snapped."

Less than a month later Steinmark was on the sideline on crutches cheering UT on in the Cotton Bowl against Notre Dame. Texas won 21–17, and Steinmark received the game ball. In June 1971 Steinmark lost his battle with the disease, and the following fall the university dedicated the scoreboard in Memorial Stadium to his memory.

100% COTTON

A LOT WAS ON THE LINE FOR THE DEFENDING NATIONAL champion Longhorns on Oct. 3, 1970, including the nation's longest winning streak, which stood at 22 games. Down by four with 20 seconds remaining and facing third-and-19 on the UCLA 45-yard line, Royal called 86 Pass, Ted Crossing, Sam Post. Quarterback Eddie Phillips connected with Cotton Speyrer 20 yards downfield, and the All-America end

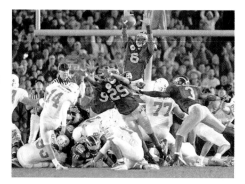

With a game-winning field goal in the 2005 Rose Bowl, Mangum (14) took his place in the line of Longhorns heroes, including the inimitable Layne (41).

Steinmark inspired his teammates (including Street, above) on the sideline at the 1970 Cotton Bowl. The next season Speyrer (left) helped to beat 13th-ranked UCLA.

sprinted the remaining 25 yards into the end zone with 12 seconds on the clock. Texas avoided the upset against the No. 13 Bruins, 20–17, and extended the winning streak, which would reach 30 games.

EARL'S BULL RUN

AS RUNNING BACK EARL CAMPBELL REMEMBERS IT, HE really did run straight into Bevo during the Houston game in 1977. "Before I knew it, I was all up on Bevo," he told *Texas Monthly* in 2001. "But I didn't mean to. I couldn't stop." He recalls hitting the longhorn in the left flank. "Bevo went down, a cameraman went down, and I did too." All parties survived the incident, and Campbell ended up rushing for 173 yards and three touchdowns that day. He finished the season with 1,744 yards and claimed the program's first Heisman Trophy. The university retired his number 20 jersey in 1979.

STAKING THEIR CLAIM

THE LONGHORNS HAD WON 25 SOUTHWEST CONFERENCE championships, but this was a new league with new opponents. Texas finished the 1996 regular season 7–4, but in that inaugural year of the Big 12 Conference the Longhorns finished with a statement, winning the title game against No. 3 Nebraska in dramatic fashion on Dec. 7. Quarterback James Brown rolled left from his own 28 on fourth down with 2:40 remaining and found tight end Derek Lewis for a 61-yard play that helped set up a touchdown to put the game out of reach, 37–27.

A RUN FOR THE RECORD

IN THE FIRST QUARTER HE NEEDED ONLY 11 YARDS TO break Tony Dorsett's 22-year-old NCAA career rushing record, but Ricky Williams broke a tackle at the line of scrimmage, sprinted 60 yards down the left sideline and dragged a Texas A&M defender into the end zone with him to help give Texas a 10–0 lead over the sixth-ranked Aggies on Nov. 27, 1998. "It was just vintage Ricky," Texas center Russell Gaskamp said after the game. Williams racked up 259 yards on 44 carries, ending the day with 6,279 yards to Dorsett's 6,082. Texas upset the Aggies in Austin that day, 26–24, and Williams went on to win the Heisman.

HE ROSE TO THE OCCASION

WITH A 12–0 LOSS TO OKLAHOMA AS THE ONLY BLEMISH on their 2004 record, the Longhorns received an at-large bid to play Michigan in the Rose Bowl. It was the program's first trip to Pasadena and first appearance in a BCS bowl. With two seconds left and Texas down by two, kicker Dusty Mangum trotted onto the field with a chance to kick a 37-yard field goal to win the game. The Wolverines tried to ice the senior walk-on by calling two timeouts, and it almost worked: The kick slipped just inside the right upright, giving Texas the win in the first meeting between the two programs. "It's something I've dreamed about," Mangum said after the victory. "To come down to a pressure kick—why not?"

FOREVER YOUNG'S

IT MAY HAVE TAKEN 35 YEARS, BUT AFTER VINCE YOUNG sprinted for the right corner of the end zone on fourth-and-five against USC on Jan. 4, 2006, the Longhorns were once again national champions, having beaten the Trojans 41–38 with Young's two-point conversion. The teams had traded scores since the first quarter, but the Longhorns found themselves down 38–26 with less than seven minutes remaining in the game. Young kept his cool; after all, the Texas quarterback had stood on the same field in Pasadena 12 months and three days earlier, after defeating Michigan in the Rose Bowl, and said his team would be back the following year. Just as he had predicted, Young and the Longhorns returned and earned the BCS's national championship trophy. "Don't y'all think that's beautiful?" Young asked the thousands of orange-clad fans who had remained in the stadium. "It's coming home—all the way to Austin, Texas, baby." □

T H E   G

A LOOK BACK IN WONDER AT 10 OF THE
MAKE TEXAS LONGHORNS FOOTBALL THE

HISTORIC VICTORIES THAT HELPED
POWERHOUSE PROGRAM IT IS TODAY

In the latest of the greatest, Vince Young sprinted to the 2005 BCS title • • photograph by ROBERT BECK

TEXAS 15 OKLAHOMA 14

WITH A SECOND-YEAR COACH AND SOME HOMEGROWN TALENT AT
LAST, TEXAS FINALLY BEAT OKLAHOMA | BY ROY TERRELL

AFTER SIX AGONIZING YEARS TEXANS NEED NO LONGER AVERT THEIR EYES.
On the afternoon of Oct. 11 a long-overdue account was settled at the Cotton Bowl in
Dallas. Texas beat Oklahoma 15–14 to right all the injustices of the recent past. ¶ Football
is more than a game in Texas; it is a way of life. The humiliation that Oklahoma has piled on

Texas at the annual game at the Cotton Bowl in recent years can be compared to the memories of Santa Ana and the Alamo. Maybe even worse. It is one thing to lose honorably to a foreigner but something else when treachery plays a part. Oklahoma, during those past six years, was beating Texas with Texans.

Until Bud Wilkinson's formula for football victory first began to flourish at Oklahoma in 1952, this rugged old Southwestern rivalry had been a mighty one-sided affair. Texas had won 30 and lost only 14 against the rivals from across the Red River. Since the Texas victory in '51, however, Oklahoma had won 68 of its 72 games and beaten Texas without serious difficulty. One way the Sooners accomplished all this was by employing some of the finest athletic talent raised in Texas. On this year's Oklahoma roster, for instance, 21 come from Texas, eight of them members of the first two teams. The Texas football fan does not appreciate his own kith and kin going abroad—and then returning to help humiliate the home folks.

Well, all that was ended this year. "We don't have the speed to be spectacular," said the Longhorns' second-year coach, Darrell Royal, the night before the game. Then this very impressive young man, who once played quarterback under Wilkinson at Oklahoma, had to grin: "But these kids sure like to play football; they'll tee off against anybody."

Though Royal arrived in Austin only a little over a year ago, his teams are already characterized by toughness and determination and a liking for knocking people down. In Dallas they started knocking Sooners down at the kickoff

and didn't quit until the final gun. Ahead 8–0 in the first half, Texas fell behind 14–8 early in the fourth quarter, but never let up. And while the entire Longhorns line—James Shillingburg, Arlis Parkhurst, Patrick Padgett, Johnny Jones, Robert Bryant, Maurice Doke and all the others down through Royal's first two units—smashed Oklahoma's famed speed with a ferocity that sent loud, crunching noises all the way up to section 127 there on the rim of the sky, it was the ghostlike figure of a young man named Vince Matthews that won the game.

One of the great passers in Texas schoolboy history four years before, Matthews had started out like a house afire at Texas, only to be sidelined by a series of knee injuries. He was the team's forgotten man. But Royal, knowing that his starting quarterback, Bobby Lackey, was not the passer needed to rally the Longhorns against OU, reached back into the past and put Matthews in with 6:50 remaining. When Matthews finished firing late in the fourth quarter, he had hit 8 out of 10 for 123 yards. The most important completions, by far, were the six that triggered Texas's 74-yard march to the winning score. With the ball on Oklahoma's seven, Royal pulled Matthews out, sent Lackey in with one play—a quick pass to end Bob Bryant—and the game was tied. Lackey, who is quite a football player himself, then kicked the winning point.

"Maybe the best thing about this," said Royal, "is that now they'll have a little more trouble coming down here and talking our kids into crossing that river." □

From SPORTS ILLUSTRATED, *October 20, 1958*

With 6:50 remaining, Texas staged a 74-yard drive that was capped by Bryant's TD reception
(left). It was clear that Royal (above) had the Longhorns on the rise. ◄ *Photographs by* MARVIN E. NEWMAN

TEXAS 7   ARKANSAS 3

THE BATTLE BETWEEN TWO UNDEFEATED TOP 10 TEAMS WASN'T
DECIDED UNTIL THE FINAL PLAY | BY WALTER BINGHAM

IT WASN'T MANY YEARS AGO THAT A GAME BETWEEN TEXAS AND ARKANSAS was just another line in the Sunday papers. Then in 1957 Texas hired Darrell Royal, and a year later Arkansas hired Frank Broyles. Since then the two coaches have dominated the Southwest Conference with their energy, imagination and keen sense of public relations.

Arkansas has now won or shared the conference title for the last three years. On the two occasions it shared the title, the cowinner was Texas. This season both teams, clearly the dominant powers in the conference, won their first four games, setting the stage for their crucial clash at Austin on Oct. 20.

The two coaches are as similar in looks, background and personality as the sound of their last names. Broyles is 37, has reddish hair, was a star quarterback at Georgia Tech, has his own TV show, doesn't smoke, doesn't drink and plays golf in the mid-70s, not quite as well, he says, as Darrell Royal. Royal is 38, has reddish hair, was a star quarterback at Oklahoma, has his own TV show, doesn't smoke, doesn't drink and plays golf in the mid-70s, not quite as well, he says, as Frank Broyles.

Royal and Broyles are good friends, and they often play golf together. They both belong to the coaches' committee that each week ranks the nation's top teams. In the week before they would face each other in Austin, with Texas ranked first, Broyles freely admitted that first was where he picked the Longhorns. Arkansas was ranked sixth, but it received one first-place vote. Royal just grinned.

It was a week of psychological warfare. Everything each said or did was suspect and subject to scrutiny in the papers. When they weren't trying to outpsych one another, Royal and Broyles were trying to figure out how to stop the other's attack. The Texas plan, simply, was to keep Arkansas's high-geared offense from going wide, which meant trying to contain the sprint-out pass-run options of quarterback Billy Moore. Broyles, meanwhile, was worried about every phase of Texas's operation, but what probably worried him most was

the rugged Texas defense, of which a major part was Ernie Koy Jr. A sophomore, Koy is one of the best punters in the country, averaging more than 40 yards a kick, and his ability to kick the ball quickly, yet high and far, has lifted Texas out of several holes.

Football games last an hour—which in the end was a lucky thing for Royal and Texas. One minute short of that hour against Arkansas, Texas was in jeopardy of losing a whole bundle—the game, its ranking as the nation's top team and, most probably, the Southwest Conference title. But with only 36 seconds left to play, a bulldog of a tailback named Tommy Ford cracked into the Arkansas line for three precious yards and the touchdown that gave Texas the game, 7–3.

Even as Ford lay in the end zone, the whole world seemed to explode. Cannons went off. Cushions flew through the air. Bugles blared, horns honked and drums banged. People—and there were more than 64,000 of them in the stadium—screamed and yelled and slugged each other happily while a sad few, Arkansas footers, cried and quietly cut their throats. Texas was the winner and still heavyweight champion of college football.

With the crack of the final gun, Royal, surrounded by a mob, fought his way toward midfield. Broyles, surrounded by no one, was there to meet him. The two shook hands in the traditional manner, no more, no less. Then Royal began trading hugs and punches with his assistant coaches as the whole group was borne off toward the dressing room. Broyles watched him an instant, turned and walked away, his right hand idly tucking in his shirttail.   □

From SPORTS ILLUSTRATED, *October 29, 1962*

Ford, who would be named All-America a year later, bulled his way to the game's only touchdown (left); Koy (above) was a defensive weapon for Royal's Longhorns. ◄ *Photographs by* FRANK SCHERSCHEL

TEXAS 21 ALABAMA 17

THE LONGHORNS' UNEXPECTED FIREPOWER ON OFFENSE SURPRISED
THE COUNTRY'S NUMBER 1 TEAM | BY JOHN UNDERWOOD

ON A NIGHT WHEN THE ALABAMA FOOTBALL TEAM WAS PARTAKING OF ONE of the specially planned distractions—a Miami Beach hotel floor show—that make the Orange Bowl game such a beguiler of flesh and spirit, Mel Torme, pop singer of reputation but no known mystic powers, suggested a song of dedication for the team. "It's the wrong time, and the wrong place," he crooned and got a big laugh. It was the season to twit Alabama, because the Crimson Tide was the Orange Bowl's star attraction, the No. 1 team in the nation, taking on fifth-ranked Texas. "Alabama players don't know the meaning of the word *fear*," said a luncheon speaker at the Columbus Hotel. "Can't spell it either." Another big laugh. Except that for Alabama, fear was ultimately no laughing matter. By the end of the week the Crimson Tide still did

not have the least knowledge of the meaning of the word, but it could define frustration in five languages. In a game of marvelous excitement, great lasting suspense and total departure from form, Texas knocked off favored Alabama 21–17. The victory was deserved, but the circumstances had an air of unreality for both sides.

Twenty-one points, first of all, represents an entire season of scoring for opponents of an Alabama football team. A 69-yard touchdown pass against the Tide secondary might happen, but only in the dreams of a Tennessee quarterback or an end from LSU. A 79-yard touchdown run—well, some dreams are more ridiculous than others. Since Paul Bryant went to Tuscaloosa seven years ago, such occurrences ceased to occur. Until last week.

On the other hand, Texas's longest touchdown run of the 1964 season had consumed a breath-conserving 21 yards; its longest pass for a score had covered only four more yards. Like Alabama, Texas under Darrell Royal has been a team expert in the art of conservative victory, but generally its victories are as thrilling as the cover of a telephone directory. Texas fans once applauded quarterback Marvin

Kristynik just for throwing a spiral. Yet there the Longhorns were, striking long range at Alabama in the first half with Ernie Koy's 79-yard run and Jimmy Hudson's 69-yard pass to George Sauer for touchdowns. "Not exactly characteristic," said Royal afterward.

Texas's third score came after a downfield holding penalty put the Longhorns on the Alabama 13. Koy slanted in, and Texas went up 21–7 at halftime.

The second half belonged to Alabama's celebrated quarterback, Joe Namath. Despite being hobbled by cartilage damage in his right knee sustained less than a week before, the electrifying Namath, the best passer in college football, took Alabama 63 yards for one score.

In the fourth quarter Namath worked Alabama in again, this time for a field goal, and finally to the six-yard line on the last Alabama drive. Three fullback plunges by Steve Bowman reached the one. At the line of scrimmage on fourth down Namath thought he saw a trace of daylight at right guard. He ignored his knee trouble and disappeared into a cascade of white-and-orange jerseys. Eventually Namath could be seen in the end zone, but only after the play was blown dead.

Texas never got past midfield in the second half and made only four first downs as the Crimson Tide overshifted to the strong side to adjust to the power sweeps of Koy. But for all the momentum Namath provided, Texas had won the game in the first half and preserved it with that goal line defense.

From SPORTS ILLUSTRATED, *January 11, 1965*

Kristynik (left) led the Longhorns' first-half surge before Tommy Nobis (60) and the Texas defense stuffed Namath's last drive in the fourth quarter (above). ◂ *Photograph by* WALTER IOOSS JR.

TEXAS 15 ARKANSAS 14

AGAINST A FIRED-UP ARKANSAS SQUAD, THE LONGHORNS' GRIT—AND
SLICK PLAY—EARNED TEXAS A NATIONAL TITLE | BY DAN JENKINS

ALL WEEK IN TEXAS THE PEOPLE HAD SAID THE HOGS AIN'T NUTHIN' BUT groceries and that on Saturday, in the thundering zoo of Fayetteville, the No. 1 Longhorns would eat—to quote the most horrendous pun ever thought of by some Lone Star wit—"hog meat with Worster-Speyrer sauce." ¶ This is not exactly what Darrell Royal's team dined on

up there in those maddening Ozark hills on Dec. 6, of course. What Texas (that would be fullback Steve Worster, receiver Cotton Speyrer and the rest of the boys) had was one hell of a hard time winning the national championship 15–14 from a quicker, more alert Arkansas team that for three quarters made the Longhorns look like your everyday, common, ordinary whip dog Baylor or Rice.

Watching the emotional Razorbacks bounce Texas around on its AstroTurf for 45 minutes, one could think only of Royal's sober warnings of the day before. "They're gonna come after us with their eyes pulled up like BBs," he had said. "And they'll be defending every foot as if Frank Broyles has told 'em there's a 350-foot drop just behind 'em into a pile of rocks. If you believe that, you're pretty hard to move around."

Arkansas was certainly that. Until the first play of the fourth quarter, the closest Texas had driven was to the Arkansas 31-yard line, and most of the time it hadn't been able to get across midfield. The Razorbacks were doing exactly what their coach, Broyles, had said they had to do—stay put and don't miss tackles—against the second-best rushing team, statistically at least, that ever played college football.

Meanwhile, Arkansas quarterback Bill Montgomery, so cool and clever he even impressed that former second-string tackle from Whittier, Richard Nixon—who was on hand along with a full Secret Service detail and a 50-person White House press corps—was hurling a 21-yard pass to John Rees to set up a touchdown in the first quarter and a 29-yard touchdown to his roommate-end Chuck Dicus early in the third quarter to put the Razorbacks up 14–0

and lay the foundation for an upset.

But then Texas's little quarterback, James Street, finally got himself and his gang going. Street is not an especially good passer, and he has never been compared with O.J. Simpson in the open field, but James Street is a winner. He had not lost in 18 straight games since becoming the Texas quarterback. And now he was about to make it 19 straight—somehow, someway, in the midst of all of that chaos in the Ozarks.

On second down and nine from the Arkansas 42 on the first play of the fourth quarter, Street, who bears the nickname Slick because of his good looks, his flashy clothes and, more important to Royal, his ball handling, dropped back to pass. Seeing his receivers covered, Street darted through the line, flashed into the Arkansas secondary, slipped past tacklers and sped on an angle across the field, running for either the goal line or the presidential helicopter. No one was about to catch him. It was the first daylight Texas had seen, and Street took advantage of it for the touchdown.

He then went for and got the conversion and, after Texas intercepted a Montgomery pass in the end zone to prevent another Arkansas score, hit tight end Randy Peschel on a 44-yard bomb that set up Jim Bertelsen's tying touchdown. Kicker Happy Feller provided the winning extra point.

Hog meat? Hogwash. Royal knew that his Longhorns, laboring under as much duress as any No. 1 ever had in such bizarre circumstances—with time running out, with a president watching, on alien ground, with very few friends about—had somehow survived. □

From SPORTS ILLUSTRATED, *December 15, 1969*

Held scoreless for three quarters, the Longhorns, led by Street, got on the trail at last. Bertelsen barreled in with the tying TD (left, 35), and Nixon paid a Royal visit (above). ◄ *Photograph by* JOHN IACONO

TEXAS 21 NOTRE DAME 17

A GAMBLE IN THE CLOSING MOMENTS GAVE TEXAS A COTTON BOWL WIN
OVER NOTRE DAME AND ANOTHER NATIONAL TITLE | BY DAN JENKINS

AND SO THERE LIES A YOUNG MAN NAMED COTTON SPEYRER, ALL 5' 11" AND 169 pounds of him, ringing out the old hundred years of college football and ringing in the new, holding on to something called No. 1. Speyrer has just wheeled back, knelt, lurched and scooped up a forward pass thrown by another obstinate elf, James Street, on a gravely

executed play that will simply have to be filed away among the real treasures of the sport. For it was this gamble in those last fading moments of the Cotton Bowl—this fourth-down pass from one gutty urchin to another—that enabled Texas to defeat a valiant Notre Dame team 21–17 in as courageous a game as any two schools played throughout the whole of the century.

Behind 17–14 late in the fourth quarter, Texas—which had trailed all day before scoring on drives of 74 and 77 yards just to get back into the game—had moved the ball once more to the Notre Dame 10. It was fourth-and-two, 2:26 to play, and the Longhorns took a timeout. Street went to coach Darrell Royal. Texas was in field goal range, but what would a tie do? Make Penn State, which would beat Missouri on this same day, or USC, which would beat Michigan, the No. 1 team in the nation? Besides, Royal has always said, "When you're Number 1, you've got to try to stay that way or get carried out feetfirst."

The whole stadium was standing, and the bands were blaring out a couple of fairly familiar fight songs while the Texas quarterback talked with his coach.

Street said, "How 'bout the counter option fake to the short side?"

Royal mulled it over.

Across the way, Irish coach Ara Parseghian was certain Texas would either run wide or pass. He told linebacker Bob Olson to play the run first. It was a matter of percentages. Out on the field now, Speyrer, his back turned to the Notre Dame defense, was signaling the bench.

He was dragging his thumb across his chest in the manner of a hitchhiker. The signal to Royal meant that Speyrer's defender, Clarence Ellis, was playing him tight and to the inside. It meant that Speyrer thought he could get outside on him for a quick pass.

"Left 89 Out," said Royal.

Street blinked. It was just as it had been in a 15–14 win over Arkansas less than a month earlier, Royal gambling on a pass in a moment of supreme stress and Street wondering, "Coach, are you sure?"

"Watch for the keep first," Royal told him. "You might be able to fall for two yards. But if you can't, drill it to Cotton. He says he's open on the out."

Street went to the Texas huddle and said, "Aw-right, suck it up. This might be our last play of the season, so let's make it a good one. . . . Everybody get tough. . . ." Then he looked right at Cotton Speyrer and called the play.

Street took the snap, looked at the end coming up fast, stopped and threw. It was low, but Speyrer did his thing and made the catch. And three plays later, with exactly 1:08 on the clock, another urchin, Billy Dale, a 5' 10", 190-pound junior halfback who had replaced starter Ted Koy, hugged a handoff from Street and followed a couple of blocks by fullback Steve Worster and tight end Randy Peschel into the end zone.

In that instant Darrell Royal won his second unanimous national championship of the 1960s and firmly took his place among the coaching elite. Urchins do accomplish wonders. □

From SPORTS ILLUSTRATED, *January 12, 1970*

One-way Street: The scrappy quarterback (left) kept his team moving forward against the Irish to cap an undefeated season, then he and Royal got the O.K. from LBJ (above). ◄ *Photograph by* JAMES DRAKE

TEXAS 14   ALABAMA 12

A LITTLE TEXAS INGENUITY PROVED TO BE THE DIFFERENCE AGAINST
FAVORED ALABAMA IN THE COTTON BOWL | BY PAT PUTNAM

THE FIRST TEXAS TOUCHDOWN CAME ON A DUSTED-OFF QUARTERBACK DRAW that wasn't even in the game plan. It's a wonder the Longhorns remembered how it was supposed to go; the last time they used it was against Oklahoma—in 1980. The second, an unsophisticated thrust that put away favored Alabama 14–12 in the Cotton Bowl, wasn't scored

by one of those flashy Texas tailbacks but by a fullback—a Longhorns synonym for *blocker*—who couldn't believe his number had been called.

Until those golden moments, the first of which came with less than 11 minutes remaining, the Texas attack had come up empty. Mostly the Longhorns had shown a fruitless routine of tailback right, tailback left, followed by the sacking of quarterback Robert Brewer (seven times) and a punt. After three quarters, the closest Texas had come to putting points up was a missed 50-yard field goal by Raul Allegre.

Bear Bryant's third-ranked Tide, at that point on New Year's Day still within range of a national championship, was delighted. It had gotten a touchdown on a six-yard pass from scrambling-for-his-life quarterback Walter Lewis in the second quarter. And Peter Kim, a 5' 8" Korean who discovered football in Hawaii, had increased Alabama's advantage to 10–0 with a 24-yard field goal a few minutes into the fourth quarter.

But 'Bama, historically strong in the last quarter, was starting to flag badly. And Texas—which finished the regular season with a 9-1-1 record (as did Alabana) and was ranked fifth by SI and UPI and sixth in the AP poll—is a remarkably strong fourth-quarter team as well. At halftime, with the Longhorns down 7–0, Texas coach Fred Akers told his team not to worry. "You hold them in the third quarter," he told his defense. Then, turning to his offense, he said, "And *you* get them in the fourth."

The Longhorns' defense did as ordered, allowing only Kim's field goal with 12:27 to play in the fourth quarter. And then Brewer finally got the Texas offense untracked.

The 6-foot, 186-pound junior from Richardson, Texas, whose father, Charley, now a Dallas banker, had quarterbacked the Longhorns to a 21–6 defeat of Bryant's Texas A&M team in 1955, guided Texas to first-and-10 on the Alabama 30 and then, after two incompletes, took advantage of a Crimson Tide blitz to score on that retro quarterback draw.

Allegre's kick made it 10–7 with 10:22 to play. A few minutes later, after an Alabama punt, Brewer was back in business, this time from his own 20. Ten plays took Texas to the Tide eight, the big ones being passes to tight end Lawrence Sampleton: one for 37 yards, the other for 19. Now in the huddle Brewer called Play 24. This time it was fullback Terry Orr, whose eyes widened. "I was surprised. I was just waiting to hear who I was supposed to block," he said. The play is a quick fullback dive over right guard. Orr went the wrong way. On purpose. "I saw that [left guard] Joe Shearin had flattened his man, so I went that way," he said. "A linebacker slapped at me, but that was all." He plunged in for the score, and Allegre added the extra point to make it 14–10 with 2:05 left.

Alabama made one last charge, but Texas safety William Graham's interception on the one-yard line sealed the game. No sooner had Graham come down with the ball than Akers was giving instructions to Brewer. "Don't take any chances. I want three Zeroes; kill all the time you can, then give them a safety." Play Zero is a quarterback sneak. Three of those netted three yards, and then the safety made it 14–12. After the punt Alabama had 48 seconds in which to go 59 yards. It wasn't nearly enough.   □

From SPORTS ILLUSTRATED, *January 11, 1982*

Orr surprised 'Bama—and himself—when he broke free for the winning TD (left). Graham's
fourth-quarter interception (above) sealed the victory for the Longhorns. ◄ *Photograph by* TONY TOMSIC

TEXAS 45 HOUSTON 24

WITH A DOSE OF RIGHTEOUS ANGER AND A RAMPAGING FRESHMAN
TAILBACK, TEXAS TAMED FAVORED HOUSTON | **BY AUSTIN MURPHY**

WHAT BETTER WAY TO BEGIN A TEXAS-IS-BACK STORY THAN WITH A ROYALISM?
Former Longhorns coach Darrell Royal once declared, "Trends are bunk—only angry people win football games." With a Cotton Bowl bid riding on the outcome of the Nov. 10 game
against unbeaten and untied Houston, the Longhorns confirmed the wisdom of Royal's

edict. The Cougars had bludgeoned
Texas in three previous meetings
by a combined score of 173–64,
and now they hoped to make it four
straight but found themselves on
the field facing some angry young
men. Before 82,457 spectators in
Austin's Memorial Stadium—the
vast majority cheering raucously for
Texas—the Longhorns pulled off a
45–24 upset by stuffing the Cougars'
high-scoring, pass-happy, run-and-
shoot offense.

In winning their seventh game

against only one loss, a 29–22 defeat by Colorado in the
second game of the season, the Longhorns had their way
with Houston's linemen in the trenches and, against all
expectations, thwarted the Cougars' vaunted air attack
with predominantly man-to-man coverage. ("We'll play
a lot of man-to-man against them," Texas senior safety
Stanley Richard had promised. "Know why? Real men
play man.") The efforts of the Longhorns' defense allowed quarterback Peter Gardere to outplay his more
celebrated Cougars counterpart, David Klingler, who
entered the day having thrown for 34 touchdowns and
444.1 yards per game.

But nothing brought the Texas faithful as much joy as
did the rampages of Butch Hadnot, a 6' 2", 210-pound true
freshman tailback out of Kirbyville, Texas, who rushed
for 134 yards on 23 carries and scored three touchdowns.
At Kirbyville High, Hadnot scored 24 touchdowns his
senior year and ran the 100 meters in 10.5 seconds, according to the Longhorns' media guide. The biographical
sketch also says that Hadnot bench-presses 385 pounds.
It might have also mentioned that all by himself, Hadnot

evokes the glory years of the 1960s
and '70s, when Texas won three national championships and 11 Southwest Conference titles. Hadnot ac-
complishes this by bowling over
defenders like a young Earl Campbell, the Longhorns' 1977 Heisman
Trophy winner. Indeed, as Hadnot
scattered Cougars as if he were fit-
ted with a cowcatcher, it was easy
to see why his teammates call him
Baby Earl.

Texas, suddenly wide awake
after six years of torpor, is set to
reclaim the honors that Longhorns teams used to take
for granted: a conference title, a Cotton Bowl berth,
national respect. In the winners' dressing room, the
Longhorns listened to their customary postgame tape of
Sister Sledge's *We Are Family*, an anthem borrowed from
the 1979 Pittsburgh Pirates. The feel-good chart topper
failed to pacify the pumped-up Longhorns. Upon being
informed that Houston tailback Chuck Weatherspoon,
who had been averaging 107.25 yards a game rushing, had picked up just 50 yards against their defense,
Longhorns linebacker Brian Jones shouted, "Chuck
who? Weatherspoon? Try Teaspoon!"

Said cornerback Willie Mack Garza, "You hear it over
and over again, how their offense is so unstoppable. Their
coach, John Jenkins, has been talking a lot of smack in the
papers about what they did to us last year and two years
ago. Well, this is 1990, and it feels good to make them shut
their mouths."

Even in victory, these Longhorns remain angry young
men.   □

From SPORTS ILLUSTRATED, *November 18, 1990*

The hard-charging Hadnot (left) left his mark on the Cougars, rushing for 134 yards and three
TDs, while the Texas D brought Klingler to earth (above). ◄ *Photographs by* HEINZ KLUETMEIER

TEXAS 37 NEBRASKA 27

UNDERDOGS TO THE CORNHUSKERS, THE LONGHORNS, LED BY COACH JOHN
MACKOVIC AND QB JAMES BROWN, "SHOCKED THE WORLD" | BY TIM LAYDEN

AN HOUR BEFORE THE INAUGURAL BIG 12 CONFERENCE CHAMPIONSHIP GAME,
on Dec. 7, members of the Texas band rolled onto the floor of the Trans World Dome in
St. Louis, wearing their burnt-orange cowboy and cowgirl uniforms like period pieces from
the Longhorns' storied past. "Horns, 31–27, just watch!" shouted a tuba player, and you had to

think, O.K., Roy, now run along and
play with Trigger. Yet as the game's
end approached, there was the band
and 4,000 Texas fans—resembling a
rust spot on the side of a fire truck
as they ignored the 40,000-plus red-
clad Nebraskans surrounding them
in the stands—celebrating the seem-
ingly impossible.

On the sideline below, Longhorns
players howled at the disrespect
shown them before the game and
danced at their 37–27 upset in the
making. Senior wideout Mike Adams
pounded his chest with his fist and screamed, almost in
anger, "To hell with Nebraska. We got the heart." A few
feet away sophomore offensive tackle Octavious Bishop
raised a helmet in his hand and barked in the language of
the little man made large. "Nobody gave us a chance," he
yelled. "We shocked the world."

Indeed, the Longhorns, 7–4 and unranked, were 20-point
underdogs to Nebraska, but junior quarterback James Brown
spiced up a potentially dull pregame week by saying on
Dec. 2, "I think we'll win by three touchdowns." There is a
cool courage about Brown that first showed itself when Texas
was recruiting him as the state's top-rated quarterback, out of
Beaumont's West Brook High, and people in his hometown
told him that Texas would never put itself in the hands of an
African-American quarterback. "That made me mad, people
telling me what I can't do," says Brown.

So it should come as no surprise that, on game day, he
rushed onto the carpet at the Trans World Dome and did a little dance right on the N in Nebraska's end zone, just to punc-
tuate his prediction. Or that he played brilliantly, completing
19 of 28 passes for 353 yards and one touchdown. Behind him

senior tailback Priest Holmes rushed
for 120 yards and three touchdowns,
and in front of him a young offensive
line held the Cornhuskers' fierce pass
rushers sackless.

With 2:40 to play and the Longhorns leading 30–27 and facing
fourth-and-two-inches on their own
28, coach John Mackovic made the
kind of call that shapes a legacy, and
Brown made the kind of play that
crushes typecasting. Mackovic had
his team line up in a tight goal line
formation for a play called Steelers
Roll Left, a sprint out by Brown with a pass-run option; on
this occasion Mackovic put the emphasis on running and
making the first down. So close to their own end zone, the
Horns would most assuredly lose if they failed to pick up
the first down. Mackovic had often practiced this play in
his 12 years as a college coach and had used it in goal line
situations. But he had tried it only once on fourth down so
deep in his own territory. That was nearly a decade ago,
when he was at Illinois. "We didn't make it, and people
called me crazy," Mackovic says.

Brown sprinted hard left, aiming for the sticks, but then
pulled up and dropped a soft spiral to sophomore tight end
Derek Lewis, far behind the flummoxed Nebraska secondary, at the Texas 42. Lewis rolled down the sideline to the
Nebraska 11, completing a 61-yard play. "Calling that play
took. . . ," said senior linebacker Tyson King later, searching for the right body part to describe Mackovic's bravery,
". . . guts." On the next snap Holmes bolted through the
beaten defense for the killing score with 1:53 to play, and
the small Texas crowd made the Dome shake just a little. □

From SPORTS ILLUSTRATED, *December 16, 1996*

Brown kept the Cornhuskers off-balance with his feet (left), then beat them with his arm on a daring
61-yard pass play to Lewis (above) on fourth down late in the game. ◄ *Photographs by* DAVID E. KLUTHO

TEXAS 25   OHIO STATE 22

WITH A STUNNING COMEBACK VICTORY, VINCE YOUNG AND THE
LONGHORNS SET THE TONE FOR A MAGICAL SEASON | BY AUSTIN MURPHY

AFTER MIDNIGHT IN A STAIRWELL OF THE HORSESHOE, AS OHIO STADIUM IS known, Texas freshman tailback Jamaal Charles sat ticking off his big games from last year to a reporter. "Well, there was Humble High," he said, "and Tyler Lee. . . ." And then he was interrupted by Vince Young, who was coming down the stairs. ¶ "I'm so proud of this guy," said

Young, the Texas quarterback, putting a hand on Charles's shoulder. In his second game as a collegian, the 18-year-old Charles, from Port Arthur, Texas, had made several key plays in the Longhorns' most important regular-season victory in years—if not decades. "Now you've been through it," Young said of big-time college football. "Now you know what it takes."

If you're a Texas fan, you also know what it takes. It takes Maalox. The second-ranked Longhorns' 25–22 victory over No. 4 Ohio State on Sept. 10 was vintage Vincent: come-from-behind and ulcer-inducing.

Though Texas entered the game as the higher-ranked team, Ohio State was a one-point favorite. Such was the home field advantage enjoyed by a team that had won 36 nonconference home games in a row and six consecutive night games. What's more, the Longhorns were losers of eight straight games against top 10 teams and had built a reputation for being a talented squad that tended to wilt under the brightest lights. Time to bury that rep.

But before Young could rally his team, he first had to put it in a hole, and with the score tied at 10 in the second quarter, Young made his worst decision of the night. Wrapped up by defensive end Mike Kudla, he foolishly flung a pass that was intercepted by A.J. Hawk, the Buckeyes' senior linebacker. Hawk returned the ball 24 yards before Charles leveled him. That sequence typified as well as any other this first meeting of tradition-rich and richly talented programs. Momentum swung often. Established stars were as good as advertised; new stars like Charles, who led all Texas receivers with six catches, emerged.

After the interception there was a fumble by tailback Selvin Young and then another Young pickoff. Still, the Buckeyes came away with only three field goals and a 19–13 lead early in the second half.

The teams matched field goals in the third quarter. Midway through the fourth, Ohio State quarterback Justin Zwick had the Buckeyes on the move again, but Vince Young was working the sideline. "We've been through this," he reminded the offense. "Defense is going to get us the ball, and we'll take it play by play." Sure enough, the defense held; Ohio State's Josh Huston was a shade right on a 50-yard field goal attempt; and Young took Texas on the decisive drive. Trailing late in the game is not a novel sensation for these Longhorns, who engineered outrageous comeback wins last season over Kansas, Oklahoma State and, in the Rose Bowl, Michigan.

When he walked on the field with 5:00 left and with Texas trailing by six, Young had generated only six points in his previous nine possessions. If he was going to beat Ohio State, it would have to be with his arm. To the surprise of no one on the Texas sideline—we've been through this!—he pulled it off.

Young drove the Longhorns 67 yards for the game-winning score, capped by a perfectly placed, 24-yard touchdown pass to his second read, wideout Limas Sweed, who made a leaping catch while falling backward into the end zone.

After the game the victors gathered in front of the Texas band to sing *The Eyes of Texas* in the closed end of the Horseshoe—a first in what could be, for these Longhorns, a season of firsts. □

From SPORTS ILLUSTRATED, *September 19, 2005*

Young (above) showed big-play ability with his arm, reading the defense and delivering a game-winning 24-yard touchdown pass to Sweed (left) with just 2:37 to play. ◄ *Photograph by* JOHN BIEVER

TEXAS 41   USC 38

TEXAS'S DEFENSE CAME UP HUGE, BUT THE FIRST LONGHORNS TITLE
IN 35 YEARS BELONGED ENTIRELY TO VINCE YOUNG | BY AUSTIN MURPHY

UNDER A BLIZZARD OF SILVER CONFETTI, IN WHAT HAD BECOME A MOSH PIT ON THE field at the Rose Bowl on Jan. 4, arguably the greatest athlete in the world seemed overwhelmed by the moment. "Unbelievable," Lance Armstrong, clad in a burnt-orange T-shirt, repeated over and over. "This is just unbelievable." ¶ Or was it? When a player is as transcendent, as

ridiculously dominant as Texas quarterback Vince Young was against the USC Trojans, and when a Pete Carroll–coached defense is made to look like so many cardinal-and-gold pylons, the Longhorns' breathtaking 41–38 victory is easily believable. What strained credulity was that with 6:42 left and USC leading by 12 points, the clearly outplayed Trojans might actually win.

But as Longhorns right tackle Justin Blalock said while celebrating on the field, not far from where Armstrong posed for photos with a gaggle of Texas cheerleaders, "We kept our poise, put the ball in Vince's hands and let the man do what he does."

All Young did was outplay a pair of Heisman Trophy winners, USC's Matt Leinart and Reggie Bush, amassing 467 yards of total offense. He completed 30 of 40 passes for 267 yards and ran 19 times for 200 yards and three touchdowns. His last carry, on fourth-and-five from the USC eight-yard line with 19 seconds to play, went for the touchdown that clinched the Longhorns' first national title in 35 years. It also terminated the two-time defending champion Trojans' winning streak at 34 games, extending Texas's to 20, and left a loquacious man at a temporary loss for words. "I've been planning this speech for 33 years," coach Mack Brown told his players in the winners' locker room, "but right now I don't really know what to say."

And yet there were Young and his Longhorns, with 2:13 left in the fourth quarter, trailing 38–33.

It was USC's LenDale White, whose thunderous inside runs (he rushed for 124 yards and three touchdowns),

coupled with Leinart's precision passing (29 of 40 passes for 365 yards), who got the Trojans back into the game following a nine-point first-half deficit. In the second half USC had run off 28 points and never punted. Then on fourth-and-one at the Texas 45 with 2:13 left, Carroll opted to go for it. Gain one yard, win the game. "We just blitzed everyone," Longhorns safety Michael Huff, who helped stuff White inches shy, said later. Young would have one final chance.

After the Heisman runner-up moved the Longhorns 48 yards in nine plays, the 2005 college football season came down to a single snap. Out of the shotgun Young looked to pass. "I went all the way through my progression," he recalled later, "but there was nobody open." Linebacker Collin Ashton and corner Josh Pinkard blitzed, but they were picked up by the Texas front, which didn't allow a sack all night. "The defensive lineman was giving me the edge"—that was Frostee Rucker, who dived vainly at Young's ankles—"so I took it down."

Young took the ball down, then he took the Trojans down, sealing the victory.

After the game Carroll said that he had never coached against a player as totally commanding as Young had been. Later, leaving the postgame press conference as a losing coach for the first time since Sept. 27, 2003, he smiled and asked, "What are you gonna do?"

Disappearing down the corridor, Carroll flashed USC's familiar two-fingered salute. It is intended to symbolize *V* for victory. On this night, the *V* stood for something else. □

From SPORTS ILLUSTRATED, *January 9, 2006*

While the defense bottled up Heisman winner Reggie Bush (5), Young (left) made himself familiar with the corner of USC's end zone, here on the first of three TD runs. ◂ *Photograph by* ROBERT BECK

T H E H
FROM AN ICONIC COACH TO A QUARTERBACK
PLAYED, MANY ARE THE MEN WHO HAVE

Few teams could contain Earl Campbell during his four years in Austin. ▸ *Photograph by* RICH CLARKSON

EROES

WHO CHANGED THE WAY THE GAME IS
CARRIED THE LONGHORNS TO GREATNESS

HEROES

PRIDE AND FIELD POSITION

IT WAS UPON THESE TWO ROCKS THAT COACH
DARRELL ROYAL BUILT THE LONGHORNS' SUCCESS

BY DAN JENKINS

IF THE COLLEGE FOOTBALL COACH WAS ONCE A CARICATURE of a growling man in a faded sweatshirt and baggy canvas pants, he is today almost another cliché. He is young, vigorous, persuasive, militant and enthusiastic. Darrell Royal of Texas typifies the

rising young coach who has dominated the college game in recent years with his personality as well as his success. Others are Frank Broyles of Arkansas, Missouri's Dan Devine, Washington's Jim Owens, Northwestern's Ara Parseghian and Army's Paul Dietzel. But Royal's five-year record in the Southwest Conference—as tough a league as any—thrust against the light of his steady competition is the best in the country. (Mississippi's Johnny Vaught has won more often, but he plays an easier schedule.) Royal has won or tied for three conference championships in six seasons, been to five bowl games, beaten ageless enemy Oklahoma five consecutive times, never lost more than three games in a single season, never finished lower than fourth in the conference. Except for two of those furious upsets that characterize the SWC, Royal's teams of the last two years (9–1 in 1961, 9-0-1 in 1962) could have been national champions. The 1963 team is better than either of the previous two.

To accomplish all of this, Royal has built on the bricks of defense and good kicking. As a very good split T quarterback under Bud Wilkinson at Oklahoma (he was one of four quarterbacks selected on All-America teams in 1949), Royal seldom passed or needed to. He came into coaching in a conservative age when one paid obeisance only to field position. Behind field-position football was a theory that it was more important to be in the other team's territory than to have the ball. "If the other team can't score on you," Royal once said, "then you can't lose. You can tie, but you can't lose."

With this philosophy, Royal arrived at Texas in 1957. He was 32, cautious, grim, tense, self-conscious, ambitious. If he had a sense of humor, it didn't show. The team he inherited had a 1–9 record the previous season. Oklahoma had beaten Texas for five straight years and eight of the last nine. He did not even have a secretary. Was any of that supposed to be funny?

"We'll hit," said Royal coolly. "We'll find us some guys around here who want to dance every dance, and we'll turn [the Oklahoma game] into a bloodletting again."

A stern sideline presence, Royal still had great rapport with his players.
◄ *Photograph by* HY PESKIN

These words were just what the vast Texas alumni wanted to hear. So was his first year's record. He ended the season by taking a mixture of beat-dog seniors and eager sophomores into the Sugar Bowl with a 6-3-1 record. No Texas team since has had a record as spotted as that first one.

DESPITE SUCCESS, ROYAL'S LONGHORNS TODAY HAVE the same flavor of his early teams. They are alert, lean, fanatical, quick-hitting Texans who tackle in swarms and sprint to the scrimmage line as if their very lives were at stake.

"You can only get this kind of pride if you build from defense," says Royal. "We're proud of our defense."

Texas should be. In Royal's six seasons the Longhorns have made 28 successful stands inside their 10-yard line, and 14 of these have been the major factor in winning games.

"Our theory is, when the other team gets inside our 20, we attack," Royal says. "Last year Arkansas had us 3–0 and had second down on our three. It looked like it was all over. But Johnny Treadwell, our All-America linebacker, called the defense together and said, 'O.K., gang. We've got 'em by the tail now. They've run out of passing room. They've gotta run straight at us.' On the next play Treadwell and Pat Culpepper hit their fullback flush, caused him to fumble, and we got it. That fumble won us a championship. The point is, our kids believed in their defense and made it work. Man, it's fun to coach a team like that."

If pride is 50% of football, as most pep talks insist, then in one sense instilling it at Texas has been an easy thing for Royal to do. "It's a luxury to coach at a place like Texas," he says. "We're the biggest school in a big state. Why try to hide it? When a kid puts on the University of Texas uniform, we tell him that he's just naturally expected to believe in himself. An athlete will perform better if he feels he is representing the best of all possible institutions."

This (to Royal) self-evident truth occurred to him sometime during his boyhood when he was growing up in Hollis, Okla., in dust-bowl country. He recalls now how he lived in constant dread of having to wear government-supplied clothing. "I never had much," he says. "We didn't go hungry, and I'll always remember that my dad worked so hard that we bought our own clothes. But you can't kid a kid. If he's got eyes, he can look around and see that somebody else has got on a better coat."

Texas players with eyes need only look around them at the lovely, tree-shaded campus in Austin to see the results of six years of the Royal treatment. They include an $80,000 lettermen's T Room in the stadium, complete with snack bar, study lounge, portrait gallery of past heroes, all of it "done right," as Royal says, by an interior decorator; new offices for the athletic staff and secretaries; a remod-

eled press box; a full-time tutor, Lan Hewlett, whose job as "brain coach" is to keep athletes studying and eligible; new turf for the stadium; new turf and a beautification program for the practice field (Royal chose the grass); repaving and recurbing of stadium parking lots, driveways and flower beds; remodeling of concession stands; changing of the game uniforms from bright orange to burnt orange, the official school color; and new workout equipment.

In addition, Royal takes all travel arrangements sternly into hand. "I want our athletes to dress right, travel right, eat good and stay at good places. Things like this must never be an issue," he says. "All of these things sustain morale."

Royal's awareness of the image has led him to become a public relations pacesetter among coaches. The evening before every game in Austin he is host at a cocktail party for the visiting officials and press. He also rents a hotel suite for a postgame interview party, win or lose, and holds court

there with his wife, Edith. In the off-season Royal makes periodic goodwill trips around the state, playing golf and dining with sportswriters and alumni groups that now cherish each opportunity to rise, Stetsons over their hearts, and sing *The Eyes*. Says Royal, "I like those guys who are shot in the rump with orange. Good recruiters."

All of this would seem to indicate that Darrell Royal is quite the politician, but the fact is that aside from being a smart football coach, he can only be described as quite the golfer.

At conventions, clinics, business meetings or rules discussions, unless Royal is absolutely needed, he will be sneaking out to the nearest golf course. "I'll never be president of the coaches' association," he says, "because they put me to sleep when they start talking about group insurance and retirement benefits. I guess I'd rather play golf and complain about the rules."

Royal often plays with his assistants, who approach the game with the same fanaticism he does. Four of the Texas coaches shoot in the 70s. The entire Texas staff probably can defeat any coaching staff in the U.S.

Royal's assistants talk, act, dress and almost look like him. At present, they wear short-sleeved dress shirts, preferably with button-down collars, thin ties, dark beltless slacks, loafers and conservative blazers.

"I'm convinced the world is divided into winners and losers," says Royal. "Some teams are born losers. It's their history, just like it's the history of Texas never to stay down for very long. Three years ago we didn't belong on the same field with one particular team. But I knew if our kids could stay with 'em until the fourth quarter, that other team would find some way to lose. I told our kids this. 'They'll give it to you,' I said. 'It's their history.' And they did. They blew it.

"I know what it's like to take those long bus trips to a game. Eat that box lunch. You pull into the big school's campus, and its campus is prettier, the stadium's bigger, the dressing room is better. Your fans can talk it up all the

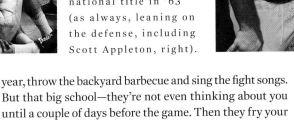

At Oklahoma, Royal (11) played quarterback for Wilkinson (that's him bussing Bud, far left). In shirt and tie, he galvanized the Texas program, taking a team that had gone 1–9 in 1956 to a national title in '63 (as always, leaning on the defense, including Scott Appleton, right).

year, throw the backyard barbecue and sing the fight songs. But that big school—they're not even thinking about you until a couple of days before the game. Then they fry your chestnuts and forget about you until next year.

"You hear guys who went to another school in our conference—A&M, Baylor or somewhere—talk for 20 minutes on why they didn't want to go to Texas. But you'll never hear a Longhorn explaining why he didn't go to another school. Put me in a room with 50 people and tell me that half of them went to Texas. I'll sort 'em out. The guy with the blue serge suit with his green socks rolled down didn't go to Texas."

A MAN OF ENDLESS ENERGY, ROYAL IS AN EARLY RISER who insists that he has never been wearied by the unglamorous aspects of coaching: recruiting trips, banquets, film study, interviews, spring workouts, glad-handing. If he is an image-seeker, he could not care less about status. "Some coaches," he says, "not only want to be the best at their trade, they want to be the richest. I want my family to be comfortable, but I

can't even read the stock reports. I haven't been 'put in on' any great financial deals by any oil or cattle barons, and I'm not looking for any. The friends I have in Texas, rich or poor, are the people I like and enjoy. Aside from my salary [$20,000], I've got a television show. I've been given two automobiles. I've been taken to Mexico for a vacation. Like others, I make some money out of talks and clinics, and I've got a book out. That's the extent of my great wealth."

Not quite. Royal forgets to include the scads of highly sought-after Texas high school players who keep flocking to Austin to play for a coach who believes, "If we can kick the ball from our 30 to their 10, that's six first downs in one play. Most teams, I'd guess, work on their kicking game at the end of practice when everyone is tired. We work on it first."

Still, Royal began last spring exaggerating the work on passing. His quarterbacks, who have private meetings with him daily during the season, were throwing 50 balls a day, as opposed to 50 per week in the past. As a result, senior Duke Carlisle threw four touchdown passes in the spring game. "Our offense looked so good, I was worried sick about the defense," Royal says.

"Last year we were criticized for being dull. Well, you make the best of your material. When we had that minnow [Jimmy Saxton, 1959–61] who broke up games, we weren't dull. Last year we didn't have him. So some people thought we were uninspiring because we had to scoop out every yard. But we were undefeated. I've tried to think what a coach wants. I guess he wants to be considered the same way all the time because he knows he can't stay up there forever. At first, our fans only wanted to win. Now they not only want to win, they want to win big and flamboyantly."

Royal himself is more flamboyant, more of an outgoing person than he was in the beginning. On the sideline he is still a tense, often grim, pacer and finger-licker. But he maintains great rapport with his players. ("He talks our language," says Carlisle.) He is in complete control of the game. And away from the field Royal has learned to take criticism about his conservative play without bristling. Last month at the college all-star game in Chicago, Royal arrived at a party wearing a tiny tie clasp with a punter on it. When he walked over to greet sports columnist Bud Shrake of *The Dallas Morning News*, one of his most persistent needlers, the writer quickly pointed to the tie clasp and said, "What is it, Darrell, second-and-two?"

Once Royal would have turned red as an Oklahoma beet and sulked away. But he laughed and began moving around the room repeating the wisecrack. The winners always tell jokes.   □

From SPORTS ILLUSTRATED, *September 23, 1963*

THE JOY
OF HITTING

WHETHER ON AN AUTUMN SATURDAY OR AT A
SPRING PRACTICE, TOMMY NOBIS LOVED HIS WORK

BY DAN JENKINS

TOMMY NOBIS WEIGHS 235 POUNDS; STANDS 6' 2"; HAS a size-19 neck and a bulging physique that gives him the appearance of a man who has swallowed a dozen bowling balls; is quicker than most of the runners he stuffs away like wrinkled suits in hanger

bags; and, furthermore, according to his keeper, Texas coach Darrell Royal, "He ain't exactly eat up with a case of the stupid." Nobis is the living, breathing, bear-hugging, stick-'em-in-the-gizzle proof that linebackers, not blondes, have more fun.

You know about linebackers, of course. They are the evil-looking guys who stand behind those groveling linemen and stare coldly at the opposing quarterback. They are the fun lovers who get just plain gleeful when they show their speed to smother a ballcarrier going wide, when they display their agility by spearing a scrambling passer before he can throw, when they get to meet a barging runner head-on, showing their want-to. They are also the players who occasionally get to drop off and intercept passes, then run in such wild-boar fashion that their coach is always pressed to explain at the Monday boosters' luncheon why they aren't playing offense. That shows, finally, that they are the complete athletes—very often the best ones a team has.

Good linebackers must be. They are the soul and heart of a defense, both physically and spiritually. They can never be tired or look tired in either respect, nor can they think tired, for many of them call defensive signals and hope to outguess the quarterback. They are such people as Dick Butkus, the 1964 season's best; and Leroy Jordan, E.J. Holub, Les Richter and Chuck Bednarik, who were all brilliant in college; and Joe Schmidt, Sam Huff, Bill George and Ray Nitschke, who became brilliant as professionals. And now comes this Tommy Nobis, who is proving for the third straight year that because of his unusual love of the game, his strength, quickness, speed, pride, instinct, coaching and ideal attitude—all of those things—he may well be the best linebacker in the history of college football.

Granted, that is a statement to rattle several plaques in the corridors of the Hall of Fame and encourage a lot of guys—Doak, the Ghost, Old 98, Bronko, Ernie—to wonder what Tommy Nobis would have done with their hip feints and stiff arms. But Darrell Royal knows.

Nobis was the latest in the evolution of a species—smarter, stronger, faster.

◄ *Photograph by* MARK KAUFFMAN/TIME LIFE PICTURES/GETTY IMAGES

"He'd have stuffed 'em," says Royal as calmly and assuredly as you please. "All he does every week is play a great game, and you can just see joy on his face when he's out there. He's done it from the first game he started, which was as quick as I could get him into a suit as a sophomore. Players keep getting smarter, stronger and faster, and Tommy is only the latest. Aside from his super ability, he's just one of those trained pigs you love. He'll laugh and jump right in the slop for you."

Nobis, who is alert and wide-eyed on the field rather than the snarling prototype football brute, jumped in the slop enough to be judged a bona fide Southwest Conference immortal before the 1965 season even began. A Texas football immortal is usually any letterman who has been out of school a year, but Nobis, apparently, is for real. He was a two-way all-conference guard as a sophomore in 1963 on Texas's unbeaten national championship team. That was a team led by tackle Scott Appleton, who became Lineman of the Year. "Scott was a great defensive player," Royal says, "but when he went one-on-one against Nobis, he got stuffed." In the Cotton Bowl game against Navy and Roger Staubach, which concluded that season, Nobis draped himself around the Heisman Trophy winner like a clawing necklace all afternoon as Texas won a laugher, 28–6. His performance prompted Army coach Paul Dietzel to call him "the finest linebacker I've ever seen in college." In 1964, playing both ways and making All-America, Nobis bulled and quicked his way to more than 20 individual tackles—most of them near the scrimmage line—in each game against Army, Oklahoma, Arkansas, SMU and Baylor, and nearly every Texas writer ran out of exclamation points.

And then in the Orange Bowl, in those unbearable moments down on the Texas goal line as the Longhorns clung to a 21–17 lead over Alabama and Joe Namath tried to take the Crimson Tide in with three plays from the one, it was Nobis again. Well, it was everybody, really, for as Royal says, "The film shows that not only did Namath not get across, but no Alabama lineman got across." But it was mostly Nobis, securing the ballcarrier. The result of all this is that when 25 leading newspapermen and coaches in the Southwest were polled to name the greatest defender in the history of the conference—a task they did not take frivolously, football being more important down there than elections and border disputes—Tommy Nobis was the winner even though his final season was yet to come.

NOW IT'S 1965, AND NOBIS IS STILL NOBIS. HE LED THE defense that allowed poor Tulane just 18 rushing yards in Texas's 31–0 opener. He made the big play, a game-

turning fourth-down tackle for minus yardage, and a lot of others in the 33–7 victory over Texas Tech. This was a game in which Nobis and Texas shut out All-America halfback Donny Anderson for the third straight year (three games: 71 yards), a feat that tickled Royal more than his collection of Roger Miller records. "He ain't drank a drop against us," said Royal, perhaps better than Roger could have. Nobis was equally brilliant in the 27–12 victory over Indiana, stunning the ponderous Big Ten linemen with his speed. But he was even more of himself against Oklahoma, because a Royal-coached Longhorn in that one is expected to put on his most dedicated game face of all. Texas won 19–0, and Nobis said, "Only thing I know of that'd be more fun would be to play OU twice on one day." *Fun* is the key word. Football may be work for some, a hostility outlet for others, but for Nobis it's a John Wayne movie, a platter of fried chicken and

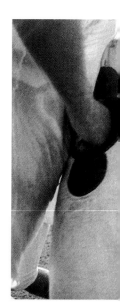

Nobis (60) averaged nearly 20 tackles and famously was just as intense in practice. Drafted No. 1 by the Atlanta Falcons (he would be Rookie of the Year and play 11 seasons) Nobis kicked back with NFL scouts and the showgirls at a New York City nightclub.

guitar music all wrapped up in a burnt-orange jersey.

With these four games behind him Nobis is on his way to All-America again, to becoming one of the precious few Southwest players to make all-conference for three years, probably to Lineman of the Year honors (since he also happens to be the best blocking guard Royal has ever had and even now plays both ways), certainly to making as strong a bid for the Heisman as any linebacker or interior lineman ever has, and obviously to a first-round draft choice of the pros—perhaps No. 1—and quite likely the highest bonus ever paid to a player who does not run, throw or catch.

But more important to Nobis and his teammates is the fact that Royal's team is ranked first in the nation again for the 14th time in the past three Nobis-spangled seasons. That would include the seven weeks the Longhorns protected the burden in 1963, the first four weeks of the '64 season before Arkansas upset them 14–13, and three weeks of the '65 season. "That," says Nobis, "is what you play for—to try to be the best. Losin' is just terrible, and if anybody's got any man in him at all, he'll go till he drops tryin' not to."

Nobis may not personally be able to beat Arkansas in Fayetteville this weekend in a game that could again decide the national championship. But, barring an injury that could result from Nobis's own hustling endeavors, a nationwide television audience should not have any trouble seeing number 60 trying not to lose. He will be where the ball is or fanatically on his way, fighting harder and enjoying it more because he is simply playing a game the only way he knows how.

"I'll tell you," says Nobis. "We're a good team, and so is Arkansas. Lots of guts and pride. But I know that whoever loses between us and Arkansas is gonna feel some real shame—I mean shame. That's the way it is. Boy, I'd hate to look at the game film on Monday and find out I was responsible for it. I just worry all the time about those films,

even when we win. I just know that I dogged it somewhere and my team will see it."

Nobis wouldn't know how to dog it if he had four legs, a wagging tail and a bowl in front of him. He is the Longhorns' co-captain, along with quarterback Marvin Kristynik, and unofficial self-appointed pride coach. Nobis had so much pride and took his football so seriously in high school in San Antonio, for example, that he got up at 5:30 every morning, rode a bus, transferred, rode another, then walked, just to attend Thomas Jefferson High (the school that produced Kyle Rote) even though another school was located only a few blocks from his home.

"In San Antone you can attend any high school you want to," Nobis explained last week in suite 160 of Moore-Hill Hall, an actual captains' suite, fixed up by Royal for Nobis and Kristynik, complete with hi-fi, TV, a living room, bedroom, view of Memorial Stadium and—soon to come—burnt-orange carpet, no less. "Jefferson had the best coach

[Pat Shannon] in town, I thought, and the best program, and it was worth it to go there."

Nobis's pride made him an easy recruit for Texas. All it took was one visit to Oklahoma. "I knew," he said, "that either Coach Royal or Bud Wilkinson would be the two best men to play for—if I wanted to become a coach. So I went up to visit OU, but you know what? I got real mad hearin' some of those guys talk bad about Texas. I guess the pride just came out in me."

He is especially fired up at being a co-captain with Kristynik. He feels the responsibility deeply, holds repetitious meetings in suite 160 with teammates to make sure everyone is "thinking right" and, more than ever before, refuses to appear weary on the field.

"You got to look a man in the eye, whether he's on your side or the other." When Nobis, who is called Rancher by the team, says this, he sounds a little like a gunslinger, which is what he resembles in the Stetson hat he occasionally wears and shirts that won't button around his mighty neck. "Look him in the eye and let him know you're ready," he says. "When I call a defense, I stare at our guys the best I know how to show 'em I got confidence."

THIS SPRING NOBIS PASSED UP A mid-semester vacation to stay in Austin and get in the proper condition for spring training, a rite that is usually deemed as much fun for proven athletes as a lecture on John Stuart Mill. But Nobis realized that most of Royal's coaching is done in the spring, and there would, after all, be some action. "Tommy is one of those people who is really sort of unhappy unless he's tackling somebody," says Kristynik with a grin.

There sure was some tackling in Texas's spring game, in which Kristynik and Nobis divided the squad between them. Most of it was by the linebacker. Once, in a violent, three-play spasm, Nobis slammed ballcarriers out-of-bounds on opposite sidelines for no gain, and then he intercepted a pass. One of the runners he literally dazed was Kristynik, who finally got up and smiled and turned to Royal, saying, "It's true, Coach. Tommy's an All-America."

That evening, up in the press box, where a gaggle of conference newspapermen were covering the game—they do that in Texas; they cover spring games and write for days about them—Longhorns publicist Jones Ramsey was questioned on why he thought Nobis was putting forth so much effort in so meaningless a contest, why he would risk injury.

"Well," said Ramsey, "it's the only game we got scheduled today."   □

From SPORTS ILLUSTRATED, *October 18, 1965*

"JUST BORN TO BE GREAT"

EARL CAMPBELL STAYED TRUE TO HIS HUMBLE
ROOTS IN THE MIDST OF BLOSSOMING FAME

BY BRUCE NEWMAN

EARL CAMPBELL HAD NEVER GIVEN MUCH THOUGHT to being poor, had never really realized how deprived his family had been, until—in the space of a single year—he won the Heisman Trophy, signed a contract worth $1.4 million to play for the

Houston Oilers and became the hottest thing to hit the NFL since *Monday Night Football*. When the full weight of his family's privation hit him, Campbell decided to take some of his NFL greenbacks and build a spacious new house for his mother and then turn the rundown plank shack where he had grown up into a museum where other underprivileged kids could come see firsthand that the NFL was, indeed, the land of opportunity.

And so, as Campbell's fortunes soared on football fields across America during the 1978 season, his mama's new house went up. And lest the contrast between his past and his present would be too subtle to grasp, Campbell had the new house built about 25 feet from the old one, with only a large gray septic tank between them.

If anyone ever deserved to have a shrine of his very own after only one year in the NFL, that person surely is Earl Campbell. Last year as a rookie he rushed for 1,450 yards—more than O.J., more than Walter Payton, more than Tony Dorsett, more than any other running back in the league—and he led the Oilers, who had had an 8–6 season in 1977, to the AFC Championship Game against the Pittsburgh Steelers, who then put an end to Campbell's spectacular season.

When Houston coach Bum Phillips talks about Campbell, you could swear those tiny hairs on top of the coach's great granite head are standing straight up, out of sheer excitement. "Earl has gotten nine million compliments without letting them swell his head," Phillips says. "I said if he got by last year without changing, he'd survive. I don't believe he'll ever change now. Earl's mama did a heck of a job raising him."

There may be no greater tribute one Texan can pay another than telling him he must have a wonderful mama. Nowhere are mamas held in greater esteem, and nowhere are the things that mama don't 'low held in lower repute. When Campbell was going through the hazing that veterans traditionally inflict upon rookies in training camp, he was

The Tyler Rose was a picture of toughness for Texas in '77.

◄ *Photograph by* NEIL LEIFER

required to stand up during one meal and sing a song from soup to nuts. Campbell sang *Mamas, Don't Let Your Babies Grow Up to Be Cowboys*, a country and western anthem to the Texas matriarchy that was made popular by his good friends Willie Nelson and Waylon Jennings.

LIKE ALL BUT THREE OF HIS 10 BROTHERS AND SISTERS, Earl Christian Campbell was born at home in the same bed in which he was conceived. From the time she was pregnant with Earl until he was a sophomore at the University of Texas, Ann Campbell worked as a cleaning lady for some of the wealthiest families in Tyler, Texas. She did floors, polished other people's silver for their fine parties, and at Christmas she gratefully accepted the hams they gave her. When her famous son signed with the Oilers, Ann Campbell didn't do cartwheels. "All this money don't make me nervous," she said. "I was always in fine places, beautiful homes. They may not have been mine, but I could enjoy them just the same."

Ann and Burk Campbell were married in June 1942, soon after the U.S. entered World War II, and she spent the war years living with her parents and his uncle while he served in the Army in France. After five years of marriage they inherited a 14-acre plot in Tyler, on which they began to grow peas and corn, and eventually roses.

Tyler grows more than half of the rosebushes sold in the U.S., as many as 20 million bushes a year. There are small wooden roadside stands all over Tyler at which a dozen roses sell for a dollar, and there are 2,000 people who depend upon the Tyler rose industry for their living. Though the Campbells couldn't hope to compete with the larger nurseries, they scratched out a living.

"I've been on this corner for 32 years," Mama said, "and all my life I never had to file an income tax return, never had no money in a bank. What little we made on the roses we spent right here. We had to take a lot of our clothes from the Salvation Army. My kids were never crazy, though. They never refused to wear other people's old clothes. We grew all the food we needed. In the spring I'd slaughter a calf or a hog, and we'd have our beef and pork for the year."

As the Campbell family grew in number, its members in size, more spacious quarters were needed. When Earl was 10 years old, the family moved a few hundred feet to another house on the same property. Mama recalls that the family completed the move just in time to celebrate Christmas of 1965 in their new house. "But the whole time we were moving, my husband was always complaining he didn't feel right," she says. "We'd only been in the new house for four months when he died of a heart attack."

The house that was so new and full of promise in 1965

now is abandoned. Perhaps because it is raised on concrete blocks, it has something of the look of an old jalopy. In fact, there is the front seat of a car on its porch.

Ann Campbell always told her children, "If you want to be someplace safe, be in church." And every Sunday from the time he was christened until he went away to college, that is where Earl was, front and center at the Hopewell Baptist No. 1. For four years he sang in the church choir.

"I never paid a fine for any of my children and never bailed any of them out of jail," Mama says proudly. "We always had a lot of love, and I think that's why they all turned out so well. We worked together in the fields during the day, and we all slept together at night."

It seems odd, given his extreme rectitude now, that Earl was his mama's only real problem child, the one who came the closest to real trouble with the law. When Earl was in the sixth grade at Griffin Elementary School, he began smoking

a pack and a half of cigarettes a day, a habit he maintained for three years. "I used to be a thug from about the time I was in the sixth grade until I went into high school," Earl says. "I lived the street life for a while. I gambled and stole, and I used to make a pretty good living shooting pool. I did just about everything there was except get mixed up with drugs."

Naturally, this type of behavior didn't win him his mama's gratitude. "She's the onliest person in life I would steal for, or lie for, or kill for," Campbell says now. "She's a great lady, but she's a terrible person to be on the bad side of. I'm her son, and it took me a long time to get on her good side."

That ascent to grace didn't occur until Campbell was nearly 14. One evening, as he set out upon the road to one of Tyler's iniquitous downtown street corners, probably for a crap game, Earl abruptly decided to change his ways. "I never really liked the country life when I was growing up," he says. "I was always searching for something else. Then that day out on the black tar road that passed by where we lived, I said, 'Lord, lift me up.'"

ONCE SET UPON THE PATH OF RIGHTEOUSNESS, Campbell found football. He was so strong and so gifted that in his senior year at John Tyler High School he scored 28 touchdowns, leading his team to a 15–0 season and the state 4A title.

"You just knew every time he got the ball he was going to get you three or four yards, even if there was no blocking at all," says Miami Dolphins rookie tight end Ron Lee, a teammate of Campbell's at John Tyler. "And at each level he's advanced—and made it look easy. I guess you could say that Earl's just a person who was born to be great."

After Campbell had scored two touchdowns in the state championship game, the coach of the losing team said, "I always thought Superman was white and wore an *S*, but now I know he's black and wears number 20."

When Campbell left home for the first time in his life, to attend the University of Texas, 200 miles away in Austin,

After rushing for 4,443 yards and 40 touchdowns for Texas and winning the '77 Heisman, Campbell continued his charge in the NFL. His success earned him national media attention, as well as the right to soak his muscular frame in the hot tub at his new house.

Earl," Patterson said, "you're not going to believe anybody can be that honest and sincere. So you're going to be waiting for him to make a slip, for his true temperament to show through. But you can stop waiting, because it's not going to happen. Earl is exactly what he seems to be, one of the nicest people you'll ever meet."

In college Campbell never shied away from hard work, and, when pressed, he wasn't diffident about assessing his own worth. Worth, as it happens, is a concept dear to his heart. Once, when someone implied that Earl would be picking up easy money when he signed with the pros, the 5' 11" Campbell drew himself up to his full height and said coolly, "There isn't a check big enough to pay me back."

As Campbell has discovered, it's much easier to leave the state of poverty than it is to get rid of the poor man's state of mind. When he purchased a comfortable three-bedroom house on Houston's southwest side last year, he asked a contract landscaper to quote him a price for cutting, weeding and trimming the lawn. When the contractor told him it would be $150 a month, which he could easily afford, Campbell whistled softly and thanked the man for his time. Then he went out and bought himself a power mower. "Earl isn't going to waste any money," says Oilers offensive backfield coach Andy Bourgeois. "He's a most frugal young man."

This isn't meant to imply that Earl Campbell is cheap. His thriftiness is punctuated by occasional bursts of generosity, or in the case of his Earl Campbell Crusade for Kids, a long-standing commitment to making life a little more pleasant for underprivileged children in the Houston area. This summer he went on local television in Houston and asked the community to donate old books, school supplies and toys to the crusade. Campbell's fans came through with a truckload of gifts, and Earl kicked in with some lunch boxes and notebooks of his own, then handed the swag out to kids in several Houston parks.

The Oilers gave the ball to the Tyler Rose an average of 19 times a game in 1978, and he responded with an average gain of 4.8 yards and 13 touchdowns while fumbling only seven times. With a number of talented wide receivers—notably Ken Burrough, Rich Caster and Mike Renfro—the Oilers rarely threw to Campbell; he caught only 12 passes. But if quarterback Dan Pastorini calls on him to run pass patterns this season, or to become a blocking back, or, for that matter, to wallpaper the Astrodome, no doubt Campbell will.

"Anything you ask him to do," says Phillips, clearly impressed, "he's going to do it. It's very important to have a player of Earl Campbell's caliber, but it's even more important to have him be the kind of kid he is." □

he became so homesick that, as former Longhorns coach Darrell Royal recalls, he "would sit on the curb and face in the direction of Tyler."

In college Campbell took every opportunity to spread the credit for his rushing feats among his teammates. "If it were up to Earl," wrote David Casstevens in the *Houston Post*, "he would probably change the name of the I formation to the We."

After Billy Sims of Oklahoma won the 1978 Heisman Trophy that Campbell had won the year before, Sooners coach Barry Switzer offered this comparison between Campbell and his own star running back: "Earl Campbell is the greatest player who ever suited up. He's the greatest football player I've ever seen. Billy Sims is human. Campbell isn't."

When the Oilers, desperate for both a quality football player and a box office attraction, acquired the No. 1 pick in the 1978 draft from Tampa Bay and then used it to select Campbell, former Texas assistant coach Pat Patterson warned Bum Phillips what to expect. "When you meet

From SPORTS ILLUSTRATED, *September 3, 1979*

A PORTRAIT OF A CHILD AT PLAY

UNSTOPPABLE ON THE FIELD, RICKY WILLIAMS
WAS IN SEARCH OF HIS CHILDHOOD OFF IT

BY TIM LAYDEN

THE CHILDREN WERE LINED UP AGAINST A FENCE AT one end of the school playground, a ribbon of billowy T-shirts, ponytails and fourth-grade innocence, awaiting their teacher's command to begin the footrace. Moments earlier they had sat spell-bound in their classroom at Kiker Elementary in Austin as Texas running back Ricky Williams answered their many questions. (*Who was the biggest influence in your life?* My mom. *What was your favorite subject in fourth grade?* Social studies. *Do you have a son?* Huh? No.) Finally they would ask how fast could he run. "I'll race you guys," Williams had said, beaming, and at the back of the room, two teachers nearly fainted because it's not often that a guest speaker proposes recess.

On the playground Williams, a 225-pound Paddington Bear in dreadlocks and cross-trainers, stood at the center of the line of 31 kids. When nearly all of them jumped the gun and darted away, he broke into a full sprint, swallowing up the peanuts until he was alone in front, the noontime sun lighting his face as he filled the air with a little boy's laugh.

Williams is many things to many people; all of the perceptions are obvious but none of them complete. To NFL general managers, coaches, scouts and draftniks who translate bench presses (400 pounds) and 40 times (4.39 seconds) into potential wins and losses, Williams is precious. He has speed and power: a six-foot tailback who can run through a linebacker or past a cornerback, plus he's smart and tireless.

To idealistic fans Williams is the latest in a short line of stars (Peyton Manning, Tim Duncan) who exemplify what's good about college sports by forgoing the pro draft and instant wealth and staying in school.

To Orangebloods who worship Texas football, Williams is the horse that the Longhorns and their new coach, Mack Brown, will ride in their pursuit of renewed glory. After this season Williams could be the leading career rusher in college football history, the Heisman Trophy winner and the No. 1 pick in the 1999 draft.

Yet at his core he's just a child in search of a childhood, eager to please. He will return to Texas for his senior season largely because he was mortified at the prospect of calling

Williams set 21 NCAA records in his four seasons in Austin.

◄ *Photograph by* BILL FRAKES

a press conference to announce otherwise. "I would have had to get up there and say, 'Thanks for all the good times, but I'm leaving,' " he says. "I couldn't do that."

As a high school senior in June 1995 Williams got a $50,000 bonus to sign with the Philadelphia Phillies, and he sprinkled the money so liberally among family, friends and strangers that it was gone before he had invested a penny. Within two years of Ricky's arrival in Austin, his mother, Sandy; twin sister, Cassie; and younger sister, Nisey, were living there as well. Most remarkable of all, Ricky has forged a cautious, long-distance relationship with his father, Errick, who left the family when Ricky was five and was soon after convicted of a misdemeanor for abusing Ricky and Cassie.

One afternoon in April 1998 Williams lay sprawled across the floor of former Longhorns running backs coach Bucky Godbolt's family room, furiously punching a game controller in a cutthroat round of PlayStation college football. When his 1997 Texas team had beaten 14-year-old A.J. Godbolt's '97 Michigan squad, Williams tossed his controller into the air, shrieked and danced out into the sunlight. "He's one of the kids," said Bucky, who helped recruit Williams and is one of his closest friends. "That's what Ricky is now—a kid. He missed it the first time around in his life."

WHAT SANDY WANTED MOST FROM life was the perfect family. "You know, Mommy and Daddy and a white picket fence in front," she says. Sandy was 19 when she married Errick and barely 20 when, on May 21, 1977, she gave birth to twins Cassandra and Errick Jr. Six years—and one more child—later the elder Errick was gone. The circumstances of his departure are in dispute. Errick says he left because Sandy had been unfaithful to him. Sandy says she threw Errick out of the house when she learned that he had been abusing Cassie and Ricky. "When he was five years old Ricky came to me one night," says Sandy. "He said, 'Mommy, you know how you always say there's nothing we can't tell you? There's something Daddy did to me that I can't tell you, because he'll hit me if I do.' I always wanted them to have a mother and a father, but that was it."

Under terms of a divorce settlement in September 1983, Sandy was awarded primary custody of the children with Errick's visitation rights "limited and supervised by the wife due to the fact that the children are undergoing psychosocial assessment and treatment for suspected child abuse." Eight months later Errick was convicted of the misdemeanor of annoying or molesting children. He says he was given a six-month suspended sentence, three years probation and was required to register as a sex offender.

Errick denies molesting Cassie and Ricky. "Yes, there's a court record that says I sexually molested my children,

but that record isn't true," says Errick. "When a woman gets up in front of a judge and says her husband abused the children, the judge is going to believe her. But I can stand before God and say that I didn't verbally, physically or sexually assault my children. This has devastated me."

Whether from the scars of abuse or the stress of the crumbling marriage, Ricky became an angry, maladjusted child who often beat up smaller boys and girls. "I remember hitting this girl when I was in first grade," he says. "I don't know why. I just hit her. I was always mad." He underwent counseling to control his rage, treatment that lasted until he was in junior high. Despite his obstreperousness Williams had been slotted from an early age in gifted and talented classes, mostly because of high scores on standardized tests. In junior high, however, his grades slipped, and at the start of eighth grade he was put in regular classes for the first time. "All busy work," he says, "and busy work

Possessing a rare blend of speed and power, the playful Williams returned for his senior season in 1998 during which he broke the NCAA career rushing record (far right, top) with 6,279 yards and also earned the school's second Heisman Trophy (far right, bottom).

wasn't my thing." He stopped doing his schoolwork and dug himself into a hole academically until his mother begged school officials to give him a final chance. He was allowed to transfer to another junior high, placed in gifted classes again and, at the end of ninth grade, won the school's award as the most improved student. "The school challenged him, academically and athletically, and he grew," says Sandy.

Sports came easily to Williams. At Patrick Henry High he rushed for 4,129 yards and 55 touchdowns, and hit .340 with three homers and 26 stolen bases his senior season in baseball. He also ran on the 4 × 100 relay team and lost just one match in his lone season as a varsity wrestler. Heavily recruited for football by Stanford, Cal and Texas, among others, Williams signed with the Longhorns and then joined the Phillies, who selected him in the eighth round of the amateur draft, before graduation. After spending a little more than two months playing outfield for Martinsville (Va.) in the Rookie League, he was in Austin for the start of two-a-days.

One more thing: In high school Ricky began speaking

by phone to Errick, and a cautious friendship developed. At one point, after an argument with Sandy, Ricky considered moving in with Errick, at which point Sandy said to him, "Don't you remember why your father left?" Ricky said he didn't, so Sandy told him everything. He stood in front of his mother and softly wept. But he didn't sever the new ties with his father. One evening in April 1998 Ricky stood outside an Austin restaurant. His dreadlocks hung like dark icicles, framing his face, and the shiny gold stud in the center of his tongue made occasional appearances as he spoke. "I don't remember anything," Ricky says now. "That's the truth. I don't know what happened, because I don't remember. He's my dad. We get along O.K."

A SCRIMMAGE THIS SPRING WAS SCARCELY 10 PLAYS old when Texas quarterback Richard Walton pitched the ball to Williams, who hurtled toward the right corner. Senior

defensive back Tony Holmes, 5' 9", 180 pounds, darted into the seam to meet Williams as he turned upfield. They collided with a distinctive pop, and Holmes was lifted off the ground and sailed five yards backward before landing on his back.

The only startling thing about the play was that it took place in Austin, and not in Chicago, St. Louis or Oakland, where many had expected Williams would be by now, rich beyond his dreams. "The team that gets him is going to be incredibly lucky," says Bryant Westbrook, who played with Williams for two years at Texas and is now a starting cornerback with the Detroit Lions. "The whole NFL is looking for guys who can get you three to five yards every play. Ricky can do that, but he can make big plays too."

Last autumn Williams emerged from the train wreck of Texas's 4–7 free fall with a season better than that of almost any running back in college history. Despite rushing for just 191 yards in the Longhorns' first two games, Williams finished with a school-record and NCAA-leading 1,893 yards and scored 25 touchdowns. There were six games in which

he rushed for more than 200 yards, and he had four runs of more than 70 yards, all of which went for touchdowns. "Guys never, ever catch him from behind," says Godbolt.

Williams had an immediate impact at Texas, running for a Longhorns freshman record of 990 rushing yards. He did that while playing fullback in John Mackovic's complex pro-style offense. As a sophomore Williams gained only eight yards on seven carries in the biggest win of the Mackovic era, a 37–27 upset of Nebraska in the inaugural Big 12 championship game, yet it was one of the best games of his career. Playing fullback, he blocked All-America ends Jared Tomich and Grant Wistrom viciously all day, providing the time for James Brown to pass for 353 yards.

Off the field Williams developed a maturity that was as strong as his playfulness. He used baseball money to pay his mother's bills when she moved from San Diego to Katy, Texas, and then to Austin. He paid for part of Cassie's tuition at Southeastern Louisiana before she transferred to Texas.

In truth there was little reason for him to return for his senior season when, on the morning of Dec. 5, he went to meet with Mack Brown, the former North Carolina coach who would be introduced as Texas's new coach later that day. Williams grilled Brown relentlessly. *Who will be the running backs coach? Are we going to play some defense? How quickly can you turn this program around?* Brown had few concrete answers. "I was dreadfully honest with him," says Brown. "After the meeting I thought he was probably leaving."

Williams only sought a reason to stay. "I just didn't want to go 4–7 again," he says. "After meeting with Coach Brown, I thought things might be O.K. This team needs discipline; we had guys out drinking on Thursday nights last year. I told him that. I told him the team needs work. I think we'll be better."

The autumn could be extraordinary. Williams needs 1,928 yards to break the 22-year-old NCAA record of 6,082 career rushing yards, set by Tony Dorsett of Pittsburgh. He needs 20 rushing touchdowns to break Indiana tailback Anthony Thompson's career record of 64, established in '89. Texas promises to get at least a little better.

At sunset on a spring afternoon, Williams stood on the floor of Memorial Stadium, still wearing his orange jersey and full pads from the day's practice. He saw his mother on the sideline and Nisey in a corner of the coliseum. Williams tiptoed to the side of the field, where trainers had dumped crushed ice in a pile, and scooped up a handful. Forming the chunks into a ball, he rushed toward Nisey and heaved the ersatz snowball at her, a boy at play, living his youth for another day and another season. □

From SPORTS ILLUSTRATED, *May 18, 1998*

VINCE YOUNG
WILL NOT LET UP

THE LONGHORNS' JUNIOR QUARTERBACK IS DRIVEN
TO BECOME THE MAN HIS FATHER WAS NOT

BY TIM LAYDEN

A TERRIBLE MISTAKE HAS BEEN MADE. RYAN PALMER, A redshirt freshman, has intercepted a pass thrown by junior quarterback Vince Young during a summer workout for Texas players, and instead of casually flipping the ball back to the offense, Palmer has turned upfield, brandishing the ball at arm's length and whooping as if he had just clinched the Big 12 title. It is an oppressive summer night in Austin, and players are wearing only shorts and T-shirts, sweating rivers. No pads. No helmets. Ordinarily, no contact. But Palmer is weaving through teammates who are already huddling for the next play, and the 6' 5", 230-pound Young is sprinting toward him. Young turns slightly and drops his shoulder into Palmer's chest, the sound of the hit like a butcher slapping a side of beef. Palmer lands on his back, his feet flipping skyward.

Younger players stare in wonder. Older ones nod knowingly. "That's Vince," says junior cornerback Aaron Ross. "Just doesn't let up."

So now Palmer knows. "I'm comin'," says Young. "I'm always comin'."

Texas is comin' too, riding on Young's broad back in pursuit of its first consensus national championship since 1969. In less than two full seasons as the Longhorns' starter, Young has passed for more than 3,000 yards, rushed for more than 2,000 and accounted for 43 touchdowns. Numbers don't illustrate that Young is also the most kinetic quarterbacking presence in college football since Michael Vick ran wild at Virginia Tech. Last fall he rescued three games from defeat and salvaged countless plays with his spontaneous athleticism, leading Texas to an 11–1 record and a 38–37 Rose Bowl victory over Michigan in the Longhorns' first BCS bowl appearance. "He has unique abilities," says Texas coach Mack Brown, "and great heart." With Young under center, plays are never dead, games are never over.

Oklahoma State knows. In November 2004 the Cowboys whipped and humiliated Texas in front of its home crowd in Austin, running up a 35–7 lead with 1:21 left in the first half. But before the next 25 minutes of action had ticked off the game clock, Young had led the Longhorns to 49 consecutive points, putting his Vin-sane signature on the victory by slaloming 42 yards for a touchdown on a broken play with 6:57 still to go.

Young, says Simms, "is doing things nobody else in college football can do."

◄ *Photograph by* DARREN CARROLL

Young closed the 56–35 victory with a school-record 12 consecutive pass completions.

Kansas knows. One week after the Oklahoma State comeback Texas appeared to be dead and buried again. The Jayhawks led 23–20 with little more than a minute to play and had the Longhorns in a fourth-and-18 hole at the Texas 45. Then Young scrambled out of a collapsing pocket, darted right, made Kansas linebacker Nick Reid miss terribly in the open field—"I gave him a little two-step," says Young—and ran out-of-bounds after a 22-yard gain. Five snaps later he hit Tony Jeffery with a 21-yard touchdown pass to win the game.

Michigan knows best of all. In the Rose Bowl, Young rushed for 192 yards and four touchdowns and passed for 180 yards and another score. He brought Texas back from a 31–21 deficit in the last 10 minutes, beginning with his 10-yard touchdown scramble after escaping Michigan defensive tackle Patrick Massey, who had spun him 360 degrees in the pocket. "How in the world. . . ?" intoned ABC announcer Keith Jackson after Young crossed the goal line.

Tampa Bay Buccaneers quarterback Chris Simms, a senior at Texas when Young redshirted, watched the Rose Bowl on television, enraptured by the performance of his former understudy. "I knew he had ability," says Simms, "but he's doing things nobody else in college football can do."

And Young, 22, does even more. During the off-season in Austin it's Young who keeps the keys to the practice-field gate. It's Young who'll tell a joke when tension needs to be broken. ("He'll even do a little dance now and then during stretching, just to crack everybody up," says junior tailback Selvin Young, no relation.) And at the team's first meeting in preparation for the 2005 season, it was Young who, upon seeing players behaving as if they were in a nightclub still celebrating the win over Michigan, shouted, "Hey, y'all! Rose Bowl's over!"—turning the room stone silent and everyone's attention to the future.

Like Ryan Palmer learned on a muggy summer night, the guy never lets up.

IT'S COMPLICATED BUSINESS MINING THE STIMULUS of a young man's passion. In Vince Young's case this much is certain: His life changed one afternoon when he was a freshman at Madison High in Houston. Young can't remember if it was fall or winter or spring, just that he was in ninth grade and that his father, a man he had barely known, picked him up at home and took him for a ride in his car. "Just showed up one day," says Young, "and took me driving around."

Vincent Paul Young (father and son have the same name) was just past 40 years old and had spent much of his adult

life incarcerated, convicted at least six times over the previous 16 years for offenses ranging from auto theft to possession of a controlled substance. His wife, Felicia, with whom he had three children including little Vince, says he left the family home for good when their son was four. "I don't know what the point was of him coming by that day," says Vince. "There was no message. We just talked. He told me a little bit about why he did this or that in his life. Maybe he just wanted to be around his son for a minute. Like we were father and son.

"But, man, he inspired me that day," Vince continues. "He inspired me to feel like this was somebody I didn't want to be. I didn't want to do the things he did. I want to graduate from high school and college, and I want to have a wife and kids and a family, and I want to be there for them. I want to be different from him."

Vince grew up in the home of his maternal grandmother,

Young attributes his inspired play (throwing against Oklahoma, left; running for a TD in the 2005 Rose Bowl, right) to growing up in a broken home with mother Felicia (right) and sisters (from left) Vintrisa and Lakesha while his absent father (bottom right) was in and out of prison.

Bonnie King, in the Hiram Clarke neighborhood of southwest Houston. "He didn't grow up in a ghetto, but there's trouble not too far away," says Ray Seals, Young's football coach at Madison. "A lot of kids in that neighborhood go bad." In the single-story, four-bedroom house Vince was surrounded by women: Bonnie, Felicia and his sisters, Lakesha (four years older than Vince) and Vintrisa (one year older). Not only was his father absent, but his mother also was often not around; Felicia worked evenings as a home health aide and stayed out late with friends. "I always held a steady job, but I did a lot of partying," she says. "I'd be out drinking and smoking with my friends, being crazy Felicia." Bonnie worked nights as a nurse but called home frequently to check on the three children and then brought them breakfast before they went to school.

At age 12 Vince was nearly a grown man, physically, and a dominant player on youth baseball, basketball and football teams. Two men helped him develop as an athlete. Ivory Young, an older cousin who played basketball at Alcorn State, guided Vince to high-level AAU basketball teams, keeping him out of Houston during the idle weeks of the summer. And Vince's uncle Keith Young, a former small-college quarterback, taught his nephew the rudiments of the position.

Vince became Madison's starting quarterback as a sophomore—"With his talent, we decided to let him learn on the job," says Seals—and the Marlins went 33–6 over the next three seasons. The tailback was Courtney Lewis, who went on to rush for 2,711 yards at Texas A&M. "We had speed, we had power, and we had Vince," says Lewis, who remains one of Young's closest friends.

As a senior in November 2001 Vince passed for three touchdowns and ran for three more in leading Madison to a 61–58 victory over North Shore High of Galena Park in a Class 5A regional semifinal. In December the Marlins advanced to the state semifinals, Madison's best finish.

The consensus No. 1 recruit in the nation, Vince narrowed

his choices to Miami and Texas. The day the Longhorns won the recruiting battle, Vince won over the Longhorns' coaches. Sitting in his grandmother's living room, he told offensive coordinator Greg Davis that he was not only willing to redshirt but also wanted to redshirt behind Simms and Chance Mock. "I went out to the car and called Mack," says Davis, "and told him, 'This is the guy you've been looking for.' "

FROM THE FIRST DAY VINCE YOUNG SET FOOT ON THE Texas campus, there was little doubt he would dazzle teammates and opponents alike with his running skills. Even as he has undergone the customary bulking up through weightlifting, from 200 skinny pounds to a hard 230, he has remained quick and slippery. Says Simms, "From Day One, if the pocket was collapsing, he could tuck the ball away and use his athletic ability to do pretty much whatever he wanted. Not many people can do that. I know I can't."

Young won the starting job in the seventh game of his redshirt freshman season, and through the end of his sophomore

year Texas went 17–2. The coaching staff has modified the pro-style offense to suit Young's talents, adding a quarterback draw, the zone read (in which Young puts the ball in the tailback's belly, reads the outside defender and gives the ball up or runs with it himself) and several bootlegs. On many plays he's a running back who happens to take the snap.

A hopeful Longhorn Nation—and cynics nationwide—await the day when his passing skills catch up. In two seasons his touchdown-pass-to-interception ratio is an ugly 1 to 1 (18 of each). He throws from off the front of his shoulder, like a shot-putter, and that's when he isn't dropping down to throw sidearm. "We talked about making a lot of changes in his delivery," says Davis, "but Vince is probably never going to have a classic motion."

As Mack Brown points out, "So many young guys come up now through the quarterback camps, where they're taught the perfect motion. Vince never went to those camps."

"I basically taught myself to throw," says Young. "Look around—Brett Favre's arm is on another level, and he doesn't throw from the same angle all the time. I'm just trying to get the ball to the receiver."

There's evidence that he's getting better. After completing 56% of his passes for 971 yards over the first eight games of last season, Young hit on 64% for 878 yards over the last four games. He has ramped up his study of game tape and is focused on improving his footwork and timing.

Even as Young becomes a more mature quarterback, he holds on to the energy that makes playing the position fun, talking harmless trash at opponents and seeking out a big hit early in the game to engage himself. Away from the field he shares an apartment with Selvin Young. They have PS2 and Xbox consoles at opposite ends of their living room, and when they're finished with those battles they often double up on workouts, first on campus and then in the evening at a health club.

The season is full of promise for Texas, which this year is seeking its first win over Oklahoma since 1999, its first Big 12 title since '96 and its first national championship since President Nixon anointed the Longhorns No. 1 after they beat Arkansas 15–14 in a No. 1 versus No. 2 matchup in Fayetteville in December 1969. More than anyone else, Young will determine whether any of that happens. So he stays late on the practice field, fulfilling his passion and chasing after Texas's birthright. As teammates start walking to their cars, Young is left with only a half dozen stragglers to work on pass plays. When somebody shuts off the light towers, there's only the quarterback's voice, calling signals and shouting instructions in the dark. □

From SPORTS ILLUSTRATED, *August 15, 2005*

A high school legend in Odessa, Roy Williams lived up to the hype at UT, where he set every major receiving record.

THE
GREATE
LONGHORNS
OF ALL TIME

ERXLEBEN J. JOHNSON COSBY APPLETON McFADIN

OFFENSE

QB VINCE YOUNG 2003–05
A three-year starter, he carried the Longhorns on his back in 2005 to Texas's first undisputed national championship since 1969.

RB EARL CAMPBELL* 1974–77
The Tyler Rose racked up 22 100-yard games on the way to 4,443 career rushing yards, 40 touchdowns and the 1977 Heisman Trophy.

RB RICKY WILLIAMS 1995–98
The 1998 Heisman winner broke or tied 21 NCAA records, including those for rushing yards (6,279) and all-purpose yards (7,206).

E HUB BECHTOL* 1944–46
After one year at Texas Tech, this eventual three-time All-America defected and became Bobby Layne's top target.

TE PAT FITZGERALD 1994–96
The only tight end in program history to earn national honors, Fitzgerald was named All-America in 1995 and '96.

OL BUD McFADIN* 1948–50
A classic two-way lineman, McFadin was voted All-America in 1949 for his defensive exploits and in '50 for his work on offense.

OL DAN NEIL 1993–96
This 2008 Longhorn Hall of Honor inductee was an Outland finalist and team MVP in leading Texas to its first Big 12 crown, in 1996.

OL BOB SIMMONS 1973–75
A ferocious blocker, he helped pave the way for two College Football Hall of Fame backs, Earl Campbell and Roosevelt Leaks.

OL JERRY SISEMORE* 1970–72
He cleared trenches at the tail end of UT's 30-game unbeaten streak and twice earned unanimous All-America nods, in 1971 and '72.

OL BOBBY WUENSCH 1968–70
A converted high school linebacker, he recovered from a neck injury that cost him all of 1967 to become a three-year starter at tackle.

WR ROY WILLIAMS 2000–03
The greatest wideout ever to wear burnt orange remains Texas's record holder for catches (241), yards (3,866) and touchdowns (36).

DEFENSE

DL SCOTT APPLETON 1961–63
The fifth-place finisher (to Roger Staubach, no less) in the 1963 Heisman Trophy voting, he settled for the Outland Trophy instead.

DL BILL ATESSIS 1968–70
This All–Southwest Conference pick was the centerpiece of a 1970 defense that limited the opposition to just 13.5 points per game.

DL STEVE McMICHAEL 1976–79
A consensus All-America and later a WCW star, "Mongo" tallied 28.5 career sacks and 369 tackles, 275 of them as an upperclassman.

DL KENNETH SIMS 1978–81
He had 110 tackles (81 unassisted) and 10 sacks in his Lombardi Trophy–winning senior year, then went first in the 1982 NFL draft.

LB BRITT HAGER 1984–88
Texas's alltime leading tackler (499) also set the team's single-season mark with 195 stops (including 120 solo) in 1988.

LB DERRICK JOHNSON 2001–04
The lightning-fast two-time All-America precipitated spectacular collisions, resulting in a then-record nine forced fumbles in 2004.

LB TOMMY NOBIS* 1963–65
He averaged nearly 20 tackles per game during his career and was named all-conference in each of his three college seasons.

DB RAYMOND CLAYBORN 1973–76
A track champ as well at UT, he was versatile enough to play running back and return kicks on top of shining at safety and cornerback.

DB JERRY GRAY 1981–84
Twice a consensus first-team All-America free safety, Gray was credited with 16 career interceptions and 20 pass breakups.

DB MICHAEL HUFF 2002–05
Texas's first Thorpe Award winner capped off his career by earning Defensive MVP at the 2006 Rose Bowl against USC.

DB JOHNNIE JOHNSON* 1976–79
Hits by this two-time All America cued the Longhorn Band to play *The Tonight Show* theme and the crowd to shout, "Heeere's Johnny!"

SPECIAL TEAMS

K-P RUSSELL ERXLEBEN 1975–78
The strongest leg in football history set an NCAA record with a 67-yard field goal in 1977, one year after he led the nation in punting.

PR NATHAN VASHER 2000–03
An All-America returner in 2001, he also shares the Longhorns' interception records for both a season (seven) and a career (17).

KR QUAN COSBY 2005–08
Texas's second-leading pass catcher holds team records for kickoff return yards in a game (159), season (1,017) and career (1,720).

COACH

DARRELL ROYAL* 1957–76
The father of the wishbone T formation went 167-47-5 with three national championships during his 20 years at the helm in Austin.

Inducted into the College Football Hall of Fame

INSIDE TH

THIS IS A JOURNEY INTO HALLOWED GROUND. THESE 10 PAGES take Longhorns fans behind the scenes to such burnt-orange hot spots as coach Mack Brown's office, the workout complex, the equipment room, you name it. These areas are normally restricted to players, coaches, deep-pocketed donors and blue-chip recruits. But not anymore. Consider this an all-access

Hope springs eternal at the annual Orange-White scrimmage that concludes spring practice. In the 2009 edition the Orange beat the White 21–7, and afterward all of the players, coaches and fans sang *The Eyes of Texas.*

GREG NELSON (7)

SPRING FEVER EVERY LONGHORNS FOOTBALL FAN LIVES BY THE

▲ THE GAME WAS THE LAST PLAYED ON GRASS BEFORE THE STADIUM'S SWITCH TO FIELDTURF.

▲ FANS SHOWERED DARRELL ROYAL WITH LOVE.

▲ WHEN IT DEBUTED IN 2006, GODZILLATRON WAS THE WORLD'S LARGEST HD VIDEO SCREEN.

E PROGRAM

pass to everything Longhorn. For example, did you know that Brown proudly displays a Masters tournament flag signed by Phil Mickelson in his office? Or that the team tears through about 300 footballs and 600 pairs of shoes every season? Well, you do now. And the inside dope on the Texas football program doesn't end there. So come on in, y'all. —COMPILED BY GENE MENEZ

SAYING: THERE ARE TWO SPORTS AT TEXAS—FOOTBALL AND SPRING FOOTBALL

▲ QUARTERBACKS, LIKE COLT MCCOY, WEAR BLACK AND GO UNTOUCHED.

▲ THE TEXAS POM SQUAD RAISED SPIRITS—AND HORNS.

▲ UP-AND-COMERS SUCH AS SOPHOMORE JAMES KIRKENDOLL (11) HOPE TO STRUT THEIR STUFF.

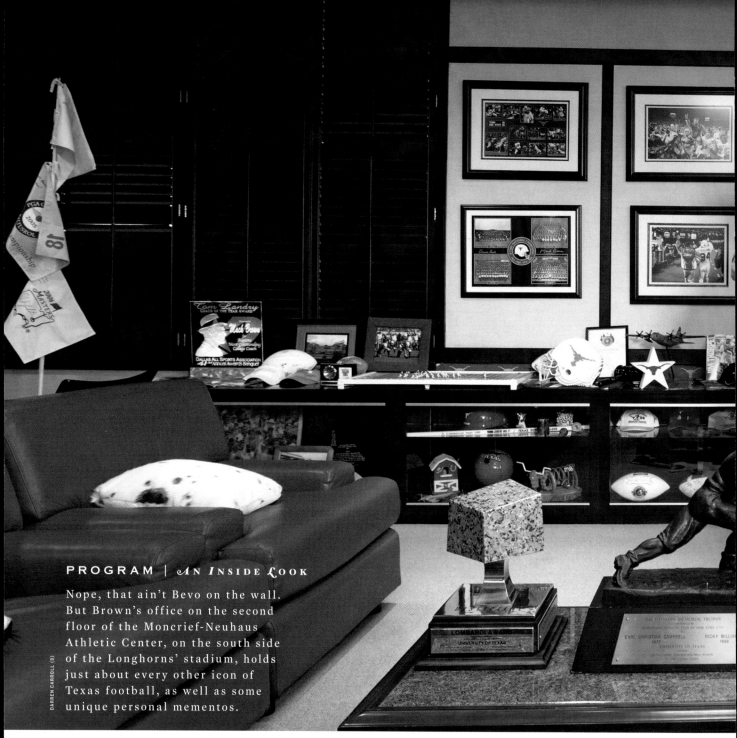

PROGRAM | *An Inside Look*

Nope, that ain't Bevo on the wall. But Brown's office on the second floor of the Moncrief-Neuhaus Athletic Center, on the south side of the Longhorns' stadium, holds just about every other icon of Texas football, as well as some unique personal mementos.

DARREN CARROLL (8)

THE INNER SANCTUM   WELCOME TO THE OFFICE OF COACH

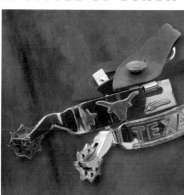

▲ GAVEL COMMEMORATING THE 2005 TITLE, FROM TEXAS SENATOR GONZALO BARRIENTOS.

▲ LI'L LONGHORN PLAYS *TEXAS FIGHT* AND *THE EYES OF TEXAS.*

▲ ONE OF FOUR PAIRS OF BOOTS KICKING AROUND THE OFFICE.

▲ EACH HEAD COACH RECEIVES A SET OF SPURS AFTER HIS FIRST GAME.

JIM THORPE AWARD
Michael Huff - 2005
Aaron Ross - 2006
University of Texas
Presented to the best defensive
back in American college football
by the Jim Thorpe Association
Oklahoma City, Oklahoma

MACK BROWN, A TREASURE TROVE OF TEXAS MEMORABILIA THAT FEW GET TO SEE

▲ THIS GLOBE HOLDS THE
MELLOW SNOWS OF TEXAS.

▲ THE 2001 HOLIDAY BOWL-WINNING
TEAM WAS AWARDED WITH THIS RING.

▲ PHIL MICKELSON PRESENTED THIS SIGNED FLAG TO HIS FRIEND
BROWN AFTER LEFTY'S VICTORY IN THE 2004 MASTERS.

PROGRAM | *An Inside Look*

From the burnt-orange jerseys to the simple helmets adorned with the classic Longhorns logo, the Texas football uniform is one of the most recognizable in all of sports. But even the tiniest points matter when getting Colt McCoy and the Horns looking their best every Saturday.

THE ESSENTIALS IN GAMES AND IN PRACTICE, NO DETAIL GOES

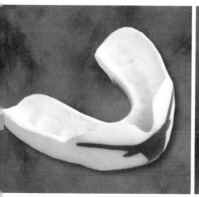

▲ LONGHORNS LOGOS ON MOUTHPIECES DEBUTED IN 2006.

▲ TEXAS GOES THROUGH 600 PAIRS OF SHOES A YEAR, FROM KICKER JUSTIN TUCKER'S SIZE 9¼ TO TACKLE KYLE HIX'S 17.

▲ NEW JERSEYS ARRIVE EACH YEAR AND OLD JERSEYS BECOME BACKUPS.

OVERLOOKED WHEN GETTING THE TEXAS FOOTBALL PLAYERS IN GEAR

▲ A PLAYER OFTEN WEARS ONE SET OF PADS HIS ENTIRE CAREER.

▲ HELMETS, WHICH COST $225 EACH, ARE ALL CUSTOM FITTED.

▲ MCCOY WEARS A SILICONE RUBBER WRISTBAND WITH THE SEASON'S TEAM MOTTO. FOR 2009 IT IS: WE ARE TEXAS.

ide and
radition of
Longhorns
entrusted to
or the timid"

TEXAS

DARREN CARROLL (7)

PROGRAM | *An Inside Look*

Named after a University of Texas alum who
happens to be one of the richest people in
the world, the 20,000-square-foot Dr. Nasser
Al-Rashid Strength and Training Center
features, among other things, state-of-the-
art equipment and a 70-yard Astroturf track.

THE CAULDRON WHETHER IT IS GETTING STRONG, GETTING HEALED

Gun Shop
Open

▲ CUSTOM PLATES ARE
NOT JUST FOR CARS.

▲ THE $4 MILLION INDOOR FIELD
WAS COMPLETED IN 2002.

▲ SPIRITS ARE HIGH
AT THE ARMS FACTORY.

EXPLOSIVE

OR GETTING FAST, THE LONGHORNS HAVE THE WORLD-CLASS FACILITIES TO DO IT

▲ LET'S GO TO THE ANKLE TAPE—IN A 4,500-SQUARE-FOOT TRAINING ROOM.

▲ THE 70-YARD TURF TRACK IS USED FOR CONDITIONING AND SPRINTS.

▲ THE PRACTICE FACILITY FEATURES FOUR FIELDS, INCLUDING THREE FULL-SIZED ONES.

THE MYSTIQUE   THE SIZE AND SCOPE OF THE LONGHORNS' FOOTBALL

▲ COACHES CAN VIEW PRACTICE FOOTAGE
IMMEDIATELY AFTER THE WORKOUT.

▲ THE SHOE WALL HAS THREE SLOTS PER PLAYER—ONE
FOR WHITE SHOES, ONE FOR BLACK AND ONE FOR TURF.

▲ FLAT-SCREEN TVs RELAY
MESSAGES TO THE PLAYERS.

PROGRAM | *An Inside Look*

Colt McCoy's headed for the training room here, but in time the 2008 Walter Camp Player of the Year—well, at least his gear—will be enshrined in a sealed locker in the athletic center, alongside those of the program's national award winners and coach Darrell Royal.

PROGRAM ADD SUPPORT TO THE CLAIM THAT EVERYTHING IS BIGGER IN TEXAS

▲ TWO BUSES TRANSPORT THE PLAYERS TO AND FROM PRACTICE.

▲ JILL ROUSE, ONE OF 13 STUDENT MANAGERS, HELPS PLAYERS SAVE FACE.

▲ LONGHORNS MEET THE PRESS—250 TO 300 MEDIA TYPES AT EACH HOME GAME.

THROUGH

FOUR NATIONAL CHAMPIONSHIPS, 27 CONFERENCE TITLES AND decades of unforgettable games against such rivals as Oklahoma, Arkansas and A&M. These are the glorious achievements that make magazine stories. In its 55-year history SPORTS ILLUSTRATED has published hundreds of articles about the Texas football team and hundreds of photographs

12.5.70 | *Mr. Blue Sky*
Jim Bertelsen ran to daylight against Arkansas in the title season finale. ▸ *Photograph by* WALTER IOOSS JR.

THE LENS

of the action on the field and the atmosphere around the stadium at Longhorns games. For this special edition we combed through our vast picture collection for some of the most striking photos of Texas Longhorns football shot by SI photographers. The result is a portfolio of images that capture some of the magic of those autumn Saturday afternoons.

Cody Johnson (31) took the plunge to score six against Oklahoma. ▶ *Photograph by* JOHN BIEVER

11.28.68 | *HANDY MAN*
QB James Street (16) ran the wishbone to a T, beating the Aggies 35–14. ▸ *Photograph by* HY PESKIN

The back-to-back national champions huddled for
SPORTS ILLUSTRATED at practice. ▸ *Photograph by* NEIL LEIFER

11.24.06 | *GOLDEN BAND*

Whether the team is sharp or flat, the Longhorn Band is always keyed in. ▸ *Photograph by* DARREN CARROLL

10.10.59 | *GROUND WAR*

Texas stoutly held the line, but Bobby Lackey's kick never took off. ▸ *Photograph by* JOHN G. ZIMMERMAN

10.10.87 | *Midair Man*
Tony Jones waited weightlessly for a pass against the Sooners. ► *Photograph by* JOHN BIEVER

1.4.06 | TURNING POINT

Texas stopped USC on fourth down with 2:09 left, paving the way to a national title. ▸ *Photograph by* JOHN W. MCDONOUGH

LONE STAR ALL-STARS

TOTALING UP TEXAS'S TOP TALENTS | COMPILED BY DAVID SABINO

COMPLETIONS

825	COLT McCOY	1,175 ATT	2006–present
611	M. APPLEWHITE	1,065 ATT	1998–2001
561	PETER GARDERE	1,025 ATT	1989–92
546	JAMES BROWN	1,003 ATT	1994–97
535	CHRIS SIMMS	911 ATT	1999–2002

PASSING YARDS

9,732	COLT McCOY	2006–present
8,353	MAJOR APPLEWHITE	1998–2001
7,638	JAMES BROWN	1994–97
7,396	PETER GARDERE	1989–92
7,097	CHRIS SIMMS	1999–2002

PASSING TOUCHDOWNS

85	COLT McCOY	2006–present
60	MAJOR APPLEWHITE	1998–2001
58	CHRIS SIMMS	1999–2002
53	JAMES BROWN	1994–97
44	VINCE YOUNG	2003–05

RB | *Cedric Benson*

RECEPTIONS

241	ROY WILLIAMS	2000–03
212	QUAN COSBY	2005–08
177	MIKE ADAMS	1992–96
174	KWAME CAVIL	1997–99
152	B.J. JOHNSON	2000–03

RECEIVING YARDS

3,866	ROY WILLIAMS	2000–03
3,032	MIKE ADAMS	1992–96
2,598	QUAN COSBY	2005–08
2,389	B.J. JOHNSON	2000–03
2,279	KWAME CAVIL	1997–99

CB | *Nathan Vasher*

RECEIVING TOUCHDOWNS

36	ROY WILLIAMS	2000–03
20	JORDAN SHIPLEY	2006–present
20	LIMAS SWEED	2004–07
16	B.J. JOHNSON	2000–03
16	MIKE ADAMS	1992–96

RUSHING YARDS

6,279	RICKY WILLIAMS	1,011 ATT	1995–98
5,540	CEDRIC BENSON	1,112 ATT	2001–04
4,443	EARL CAMPBELL	765 ATT	1974–77
3,328	JAMAAL CHARLES	533 ATT	2005–07
3,231	CHRIS GILBERT	595 ATT	1966–68

RUSHING TOUCHDOWNS

72	RICKY WILLIAMS	1995–98
64	CEDRIC BENSON	2001–04
40	EARL CAMPBELL	1974–77
37	VINCE YOUNG	2003–05
36	JAMAAL CHARLES	2005–07
36	STEVE WORSTER	1968–70

100-YARD RUSHING GAMES

28	RICKY WILLIAMS	1995–98
25	CEDRIC BENSON	2001–04
22	EARL CAMPBELL	1974–77
16	CHRIS GILBERT	1966–68
14	A.J. (JAM) JONES	1978–81

POINTS

452	RICKY WILLIAMS	1995–98
404	CEDRIC BENSON	2001–04
358	DUSTY MANGUM	2001–04
339	PHIL DAWSON	1994–97
308	KRIS STOCKTON	1996, '98–2000

FIELD GOALS

59	PHIL DAWSON	1994–97
58	KRIS STOCKTON	1996, '98–2000
58	JEFF WARD	1983–86
50	DUSTY MANGUM	2001–04
49	RUSSELL ERXLEBEN	1975–78

TACKLES

499	BRITT HAGER	1984–88
478	DOUG SHANKLE	1978–81
458	DERRICK JOHNSON	2001–04
403	ANTHONY CURL	1989–92
401	CHRIS CARTER	1993–96

SACKS

40½	KIKI DeAYALA	1980–82
39½	TIM CAMPBELL	1975–79
31	TONY DEGRATE	1981–84
29	KENNETH SIMS	1978–81
29	BILL ACKER	1975–79

INTERCEPTIONS

17	NATHAN VASHER	2000–03
17	NOBLE DOSS	1939–41
16	JERRY GRAY	1981–84
15	DERRICK HATCHETT	1977–80
13	CHRIS CARTER	1993–96
13	STANLEY RICHARD	1987–90
13	JOHNNIE JOHNSON	1976–79
13	BOBBY DILLON	1949–51

COACHING VICTORIES

167	DARRELL ROYAL	1957–76
115	MACK BROWN	1998–present
86	FRED AKERS	1977–86
63	DANA X. BIBLE	1937–46
44	CLYDE LITTLEFIELD	1927–33

LB | *Derrick Johnson*

By the Numbers

32 VICTORIES IN 39 career starts for Colt McCoy, the most by a Longhorns starting quarterback. Vince Young ranks second with 30.

.816 COACH Mack Brown's winning percentage (115–26) in Austin, the best of anyone to lead the program. Darrell Royal is a close second at .774.

37.6 POINTS SCORED per game by the Longhorns since Brown's arrival in 1998. Only Boise State (38.7) has averaged more in that period.

76.5 PERCENTAGE OF road or neutral site games that Texas has won (52–16) over the last 10 seasons, which is tops in the nation. USC ranks second at 72.7% (48–18).

Darrell K Royal–Texas Memorial Stadium

100,119 CAPACITY AT Darrell K Royal–Texas Memorial Stadium, making it the largest venue in the Big 12 as well as in the state of Texas, including Cowboys Stadium. Only four college programs boast bigger homes.

10 VICTORIES IN each of the last eight years for the Longhorns, the longest current streak in the nation, the second longest in NCAA history.

832 WINS IN Texas football history. The Longhorns pulled ahead of Notre Dame into second place last season and trail only Michigan (872) among FBS members.

48 BOWL GAME appearances by the Longhorns. That's one more than both USC and Tennessee and second only to Alabama, which has an NCAA-best 56 appearances.

LEGACY

TWO-WAY STREET

THE QUARTERBACK WHO GAVE TEXAS 20 CONSECUTIVE VICTORIES
TALKS ABOUT WHAT UT GAVE TO HIM | BY JAMES STREET *as told to Mark Beech*

THE UNIVERSITY OF TEXAS HAS MEANT SO MUCH TO ME AND TO MY family that I find it very hard now to believe I ever considered going anyplace else. When I was a little 155-pound quarterback at Longview (Texas) High, I didn't know anybody who went to school in Austin, but I did have some buddies who went to Arkansas, and I knew

a few of the Razorbacks' players. I was a big sports fan as a kid, but my family didn't have a television, so it wasn't like I'd grown up watching the Longhorns every Saturday afternoon. And I'd never been to Austin even once. What difference did it make to me where I went?

But two things changed the course of my life. First, Arkansas didn't have as good a baseball team as Texas. I was a pretty good pitcher, and I had always wanted to play pro ball like my older brother, Sewell, who had been signed by the St. Louis Cardinals. More important, Arkansas didn't have Darrell Royal coaching its football team, and after I met him on a visit to Texas in the fall of my senior year, my mind was made up. I wasn't some prize coming out of high school—the best

Street still carries the ball in
Austin, this time for his business.

Photograph by DARREN CARROLL

year I ever had, we went 5–5. But Coach Royal sat me down in the press box and said, "Look, if you don't compete against the best, both in practice and on the field, you're never going to know how good you are." That left a big impression on me, because at the time I really didn't know if I was any good or not. After our talk I was only going to be a Longhorn.

A lot of life is being in the right place at the right time, and not long after I got to Texas, Coach Royal started running the wishbone, which turned out to be perfect for me—a scrawny, scrambling kid who wasn't much of a passer. I took over as the quarterback early in my junior season, and we went on to win 20 straight games and the 1969 national title. I don't know that I would have accomplished any of those things had I gone to Arkansas. I sure know that I would have been on the wrong sideline in Fayetteville on Dec. 6 of that year, when Texas, ranked No. 1, came from behind to beat the second-ranked Razorbacks 15–14 in that season's Game of the Century.

It was only afterward that I realized how I had been a part of something much larger. Those 20 wins—and that one in particular—have opened so many doors for me, professionally and socially, in the last 40 years. I met President Nixon after the Arkansas game. I went out to Vegas with some friends and got to go backstage and meet Elvis. While we were talking, Bill Medley of The Righteous Brothers came in. They'd both seen the game. It was crazy. I hung out with John Wayne! Even in my current career—I run an Austin firm that helps lawyers and their clients negotiate structured settlements in wrongful death and personal injury lawsuits— I meet people who remember that game and our team. I'm 61, and I'm still amazed and humbled by it.

The lessons I learned at Texas were lessons for success. When I was on my own, I fell back on what I'd learned from Coach Royal—pay attention to detail; remember that you represent more than just you; keep your hair trimmed; shine your shoes; don't be late. Even today, if I tell Coach Royal that I'm going to meet him someplace at nine o'clock, I'll get there at a quarter to.

I've tried to pass his wisdom on to my five sons. Ryan, 35, is an architect here in Austin. Huston, 26, is the closer for the Colorado Rockies and was the 2005 AL Rookie of the Year. He won a national championship when he pitched for Texas, just like his younger brothers Jordon and Juston, both 23. My baby, Hanson, who's 21, played baseball at Pepperdine.

In my first conversation with Coach Royal, he made the point that only at Texas could I measure myself against the best. I think he said that because he knows for a fact that Texas *is* the best. And now, 44 years later, I know it too. □